First World War
and Army of Occupation
War Diary
France, Belgium and Germany

34 DIVISION
Divisional Troops
Royal Army Veterinary Corps
44 Mobile Veterinary Section
1 October 1915 - 31 July 1919

WO95/2454/3

The Naval & Military Press Ltd
www.nmarchive.com
Published in association with The National Archives

Published by

The Naval & Military Press Ltd

Unit 10 Ridgewood Industrial Park,

Uckfield, East Sussex,

TN22 5QE England

Tel: +44 (0) 1825 749494

www.naval-military-press.com

www.nmarchive.com

This diary has been reprinted in facsimile from the original. Any imperfections are inevitably reproduced and the quality may fall short of modern type and cartographic standards.

© **Crown Copyright**
Images reproduced by permission of The National Archives, London, England, 2015.

Contents

Document type	Place/Title	Date From	Date To
War Diary	WO95/2454/3		
Heading	34th Division Divl Troops 44th Mobile Vety Sec 1915 Oct-1919 Jly		
Heading	44th Mob Vet Section. Vol. I		
War Diary	Warminster Eng	01/10/1915	31/12/1915
Heading	War Diary of 44th Mobile Veterinary Section 34th Division From 7th January 1916 To 31st January 1916 (Volume 1)		
War Diary	Sutton Veny	07/01/1916	10/01/1916
War Diary	Bn Word S.S. Marched	11/01/1916	11/01/1916
War Diary	In The Train	12/01/1916	12/01/1916
War Diary	Ebblingham	13/01/1916	14/01/1916
War Diary	Le Nieppe	15/01/1916	21/01/1916
War Diary	Le Nieppe	22/01/1916	23/01/1916
War Diary	Steenbecque	24/01/1916	31/01/1916
Heading	44th Mob. Vet. Sect. Vol 2		
Heading	War Diary Of 44th Mobile Veterinary Section 34th Division From 1st Feb 1916 To 29th Feb 1916 (Volume 2)		
War Diary	Steenbecque	01/02/1916	18/02/1916
War Diary	Croix De Bac	19/02/1916	20/02/1916
War Diary	Croix De Bac	20/02/1916	20/02/1916
War Diary	Steenwerck	21/02/1916	29/02/1916
Heading	War Diary Of 44th Mobile Veterinary Section From 1st March 1916 To 31st March 1916 (Volume 3)		
War Diary	Steenwerck	01/03/1916	31/03/1916
Heading	War Diary Of 44th Mobile Veterinary Section 34th Division. From 1st April 1916 To 30th April 1916, Vol 4		
War Diary	Steenwerck	01/04/1916	30/04/1916
Miscellaneous			
Heading	War Diary Of 44th Mobile Veterinary Section 34th Division From 1st May 1916 To 31st May 1916 (Volume 5)		
War Diary	Tilques	01/05/1916	06/05/1916
War Diary	Longneau	07/05/1916	07/05/1916
War Diary	Bresle	08/05/1916	09/05/1916
War Diary	Behencourt	10/05/1916	31/05/1916
Heading	War Diary Of 44th Mobile Veterinary Section 34th Division. From 1st 6 16 To 30th 6 16 Volume 6		
War Diary	Behencourt	01/06/1916	23/06/1916
War Diary	Ribemont	24/06/1916	30/06/1916
Heading	War Diary Of 44th Mobile Veterinary Section 34th Division From 1st July 16 To 31st July 16 Volume 7		
War Diary	Ribemont	01/07/1916	04/07/1916
War Diary	Bresle	05/07/1916	31/07/1916
Heading	War Diary Of 44th Mobile Veterinary Section 34th Division From 1st August 1916 To 31st August 1916 Volume 8		
War Diary	Bresle	01/08/1916	01/08/1916

War Diary	Long Valley W. 20	02/08/1916	16/08/1916
War Diary	Baizieux	18/08/1916	18/08/1916
War Diary	Querrieu	21/08/1916	21/08/1916
War Diary	Saleaux	22/08/1916	23/08/1916
War Diary	Croix-Du-Bac	24/08/1916	30/09/1916
Heading	War Diary Of 44th Mobile Veterinary Section. 34th Division. From 1.10.16 To 31.10.16 Volume. 10		
War Diary	Croix-Du-Bac	01/10/1916	31/10/1916
Heading	War Diary Of 44th Mobile Veterinary Section 34th Division From 1-11-16 To 30-11-16 Volume 11		
War Diary	Croix-Du-Bac	01/11/1916	30/11/1916
Heading	War Diary 44th Mobile Veterinary Section 34th Division From 1st December 1916 To 31st December 1916 (Volume 12)		
War Diary	Croix Du Bac	01/12/1916	31/12/1916
Heading	War Diary Of 44th Mobile Vet Section. 34th Division. From Jan 1st 1917 To Jan 31st 1917 Volume 13		
War Diary	Croix Du Bac.	01/01/1917	31/01/1917
Heading	War Diary 44th Of Mobile Veterinary Section 34th Division From Feb 1st 1917 To Feb 28th 1917		
War Diary	Croix Du Bac.	01/02/1917	19/02/1917
War Diary	Steenbecque	20/02/1917	20/02/1917
War Diary	Fontes	21/02/1917	21/02/1917
War Diary	Noyelles	22/02/1917	28/02/1917
Heading	War Diary Of 44th M.V.S. 34th Division. From March 1st 1917 To March 31st 1917		
War Diary	Noyelles	01/03/1917	02/03/1917
War Diary	La. Thieuloye	03/03/1917	13/03/1917
War Diary	Villers. Brulin	14/03/1917	31/03/1917
Heading	War Diary Of 44th Mobile Veterinary Section 34th Division From April 1st To April 30th 1917		
War Diary	Villers Brulin	01/04/1917	04/04/1917
War Diary	Agnieres	05/04/1917	15/04/1917
War Diary	Chelers	16/04/1917	21/04/1917
War Diary	Tilloy Les Hermaville	22/04/1917	24/04/1917
War Diary	Larresset	25/04/1917	30/04/1917
Heading	War Diary Of 44th M.V.S. 34th Division From 1.5.17 To 31.5.17		
War Diary	Larresset	01/05/1917	02/05/1917
War Diary	Le Cauroy	03/05/1917	29/05/1917
War Diary	Couturelle	30/05/1917	30/05/1917
War Diary	Laresset	31/05/1917	31/05/1917
Heading	War Diary Of 44th Mobile Veterinary Section 34th Division From June 1st 1917 To June 30th 1917 Vol 18		
War Diary	Laresset	01/06/1917	03/06/1917
War Diary	G.A. 14 Central	04/06/1917	22/06/1917
War Diary	Tilloy-Les Hermaville	23/06/1917	30/06/1917
Heading	War Diary Of 44th M.V.S. 34th Division. From July 1st 1917 To July 31st 1917 Vol 19		
War Diary	Tilloy-Les-Hermaville	01/04/1917	06/07/1917
War Diary	Quinconce	07/07/1917	09/07/1917
War Diary	G. 22. Cent	10/07/1917	31/07/1917
Heading	War Diary Of 44th Mobile Veterinary. Section. 34th Division From 1st August 1917 To 31st August 1917		
War Diary	K. 22. C.	01/08/1917	31/08/1917

Heading	War Diary Of 44th Mobile Veterinary Section 34th Division. From Sept 1st 1917 To Sept. 30th 1917		
War Diary	K.22.C.	01/09/1917	15/09/1917
War Diary	Vraignes	16/09/1917	29/09/1917
War Diary	Peronne	30/09/1917	30/09/1917
Heading	War Diary Of 44 M.V.S. 34 Division From Oct 1st 1917 to Oct 31st 1917 Vol 22		
War Diary	Bapaume	01/10/1917	08/10/1917
War Diary	Proven	09/10/1917	14/10/1917
War Diary	A.9.c. 7.5	15/10/1917	15/10/1917
War Diary	A I6.a. Cent	16/10/1917	17/10/1917
War Diary	A 20.a 22	18/10/1917	29/10/1917
War Diary	Achiet-Le-Petit	30/10/1917	30/10/1917
War Diary	Boisleaux-Au-Mont	31/10/1917	31/10/1917
Heading	War Diary Of 44th M.V.S. 34th Division From 1.11.17 To 30.11.17		
War Diary	Boisleux Au-Mont.	01/11/1917	30/11/1917
Heading	War Diary Of 44th M.V.S. 34th Division From 1.12.17 To 31.12.17		
War Diary	S. 16. a 8, 9 Sheet 51 B.	01/12/1917	31/12/1917
Heading	War Diary Of 44th M.V.S. 34th Division From Jan 1st 1918 To Jan 31st 1918		
War Diary	S 16. a. 8.9	01/01/1918	31/01/1918
Heading	War Diary Of 44th Mobile Vety Section 34th Division From 1.2.18 To 28.2.1918 Vol 26		
War Diary	Ervillers	01/02/1918	09/02/1918
War Diary	Berles-Au Bois	10/02/1918	10/02/1918
War Diary	Le-Cauroy	11/02/1918	28/02/1918
Heading	War Diary Of 44th Mobile Vety Section 34th Division From 1.5.18 To 31.3.18		
War Diary	Le Cauroy	01/03/1918	02/03/1918
War Diary	St. Amand	03/03/1918	03/03/1918
War Diary	Boiry St Rectrude	04/03/1918	22/03/1918
War Diary	Douchy Les Ayette	23/03/1918	24/03/1918
War Diary	Bavincourt	25/03/1918	25/03/1918
War Diary	Etree Wamin	26/03/1918	26/03/1918
War Diary	La Neuville	27/03/1918	27/03/1918
War Diary	Valhuon	28/03/1918	28/03/1918
War Diary	La-Pugnoy	29/03/1918	29/03/1918
War Diary	Estaires	30/03/1918	30/03/1918
War Diary	Le-Kirlem	31/03/1918	31/03/1918
Heading	War Diary Of 44th M V S 34th Div From 1.4.18 To 30.4.18 Vol 28		
War Diary	Le Kirlem	01/04/1918	09/04/1918
War Diary	Blanche Maison	10/04/1918	10/04/1918
War Diary	Petit. Sec Bois	11/04/1918	11/04/1918
War Diary	Morebecque	13/04/1918	13/04/1918
War Diary	Godwaersvelde	14/04/1918	22/04/1918
War Diary	St. Jans-Ter-Biezen	23/04/1918	29/04/1918
War Diary	Watou	30/04/1918	30/04/1918
Heading	War Diary of 44th M V S 34th Division From 1.5.18 To 31.5.18 Vol 29		
War Diary	Watou	01/05/1918	12/05/1918
War Diary	Les Cloches	13/05/1918	13/05/1918
War Diary	Nielles-Les Blequin	14/05/1918	31/05/1918

Heading	War Diary Of 44th M.V.S. 34th Division From 1.6.1918 To 30.6.1918 Vol 30		
War Diary	Nielles Les-Blequin	01/06/1918	17/06/1918
War Diary	Samer	18/06/1918	28/06/1918
War Diary	Elnes	29/06/1918	29/06/1918
War Diary	St. Momelin	30/06/1918	30/06/1918
Heading	War Diary of 44th M.V.S. 34th Division From 1.7.1918 To 31.7.1918 Vol 31		
War Diary	F 13 A Cent Sheet. 27	17/07/1918	17/07/1918
War Diary	On Train	18/07/1918	18/07/1918
War Diary	Senlis	19/07/1918	19/07/1918
War Diary	Largny	20/07/1918	21/07/1918
War Diary	Vivieres	22/07/1918	22/07/1918
War Diary	Montgorert Longpont Rd	23/07/1918	29/07/1918
War Diary	Chouy	30/07/1918	31/07/1918
War Diary	Wylder	01/07/1918	02/07/1918
War Diary	Rousbrugge	03/07/1918	03/07/1918
War Diary	F 13 D Cent Sheet 27	04/07/1918	16/07/1918
Heading	War Diary Of 44th M.V.S. 34th Division From 1.8.1918 To 31.8.1918		
War Diary	Chouy	01/08/1918	03/08/1918
War Diary	Billy-Sur-Ourcq	04/08/1918	04/08/1918
War Diary	Thury	05/08/1918	05/08/1918
War Diary	Ormoy	06/08/1918	06/08/1918
War Diary	On Train	07/08/1918	07/08/1918
War Diary	Esquelbecq	08/08/1918	21/08/1918
War Diary	F 13 d Cent Sheet 27	22/08/1918	30/08/1918
War Diary	27/K 26 06 32	31/08/1918	31/08/1918
War Diary	Chouy	01/08/1918	03/08/1918
War Diary	Billy Sur Ourcq	04/08/1918	04/08/1918
War Diary	Thury	05/08/1918	05/08/1918
War Diary	Ormoy	06/08/1918	06/08/1918
War Diary	Esquelbecq	08/08/1918	21/08/1918
War Diary	F 13 D Cent	22/08/1918	31/08/1918
Heading	War Diary Of 44th M.V.S. 34th Div. From 1.9.1918 To 30.9.1918 Vol 33		
War Diary	27/K 26 D 32	01/09/1918	02/09/1918
War Diary	V 34 B 07	03/09/1918	09/09/1918
War Diary	L 34 B 07	10/09/1918	17/09/1918
War Diary	R 4 D 96 Sheet 27	18/09/1918	10/10/1918
War Diary	H. 36. d. 0.9. (Sheet 28)	11/10/1918	17/10/1918
War Diary	K. 31 13.2.2 (Sheet 28)	18/10/1918	18/10/1918
War Diary	K. 31. 4.2.8 (Sheet 28)	19/10/1918	20/10/1918
War Diary	Q 5. C.1.1. (Sheet 28)	21/10/1918	22/10/1918
War Diary	Lauwe (Sheet 29)	23/10/1918	28/10/1918
War Diary	H. 5 C.1.0 (Sheet 29)	29/10/1918	31/10/1918
Heading	War Diary Of 44th M V S 34th Div From 1.11.1918 To 30.11.1918 Vol 36		
War Diary	Harlebeke	01/11/1918	03/11/1918
War Diary	Moorseele	04/11/1918	15/11/1918
War Diary	Watripoint	16/11/1918	18/11/1918
War Diary	Lessines	19/11/1918	12/12/1918
War Diary	Soignies	13/12/1918	16/12/1918
War Diary	Courcelles	17/12/1918	18/12/1918
War Diary	Chatelet	19/12/1918	19/12/1918
War Diary	Sart. St. Laurant	20/12/1918	24/12/1918

War Diary	Floreffe	25/12/1918	31/12/1918
Heading	War Diary Of 44th M.V.S.		
War Diary	Floreffe	01/01/1919	25/01/1919
War Diary	Siegburg	26/01/1919	31/01/1919
Heading	War Diary Of 44 M V S Month Ending Feb. 28.1919		
War Diary	Seigburg	01/02/1919	28/02/1919
Heading	War Diary Unit 44. M.V.S. Month Ending March 31st 1919		
War Diary	Siegburg	01/03/1919	30/04/1919
Heading	War Diary Of 44th M.V.S. East Division For Month. Ending April 30 1919		
War Diary	Siegburg	01/04/1919	30/04/1919
Heading	War Diary Of 44th M V S Month Ending May 1919		
War Diary	Siegburg	01/05/1919	31/05/1919
Heading	War Diary Of 44 M V S For Month Ending June 30 1919		
War Diary	Siegburg	01/06/1919	30/06/1919
Heading	War Diary Of 44 M.V.S. For Month Ending. July. 1919		
War Diary	Siegburg	01/07/1919	31/07/1919

90 gm / 2454 (3)

50 gm / 2454 (3)

34TH DIVISION
DIVL TROOPS

3

44TH MOBILE VETY SECN.
~~JAN 1916 — DEC 1918~~

1915 OCT — 1919 JLY

LLD hab: ver Lectoris.

Vol. I

Jan '16
Dec '16

9 ³⁴

WAR DIARY
INTELLIGENCE SUMMARY

4 MMVS

Army Form C.2118
26 MAY 1919
ROYAL ARMY VET. CORPS.

DUPL

Instructions regarding War Diaries and Intelligence Summaries are contained in F. S. Regs., Part II. and the Staff Manual respectively. Title pages will be prepared in manuscript.

(Erase heading not required.)

Place	Date	Hour	Summary of Events and Information	Remarks and references to Appendices
WARMINSTER	4.10.15		Arrived at Warminster Station at 6.2 P.M. from Woolwich with No 4th Mobile Veterinary Section comprising 2 Sgts. 2 Cpls & 20 men. Marched to Greenhill Sutton Veny, and reported arrival to A.D.V.S. 3rd Division. Men billeted in Huts 30. Camp No 6.	
"	5.10.15		Arrangements with Capt Cotton D.C. 232 6OAS6 to let men mess with his men. Indented on 9.10.9.5 for general equipment for Section 1 on A.D.V.S. for Veterinary S/Sgt Inspected myn. drill parade all ranks 9.30 am, and gave them 2½ hours dismounted drill. Instruction lecture to all ranks 2.15 P.M on Appendix 1. Part 1 Standing orders A.V.C. 1916.	
"	6.10.15		2½ hours dismounted drill to all ranks. Lecture to all ranks 2.15 P.M on Appendix 1 Part 1 Standing Orders A.V.C. Stable management	
"	7.10.15		Routine as yesterday. Lecture Para I. II Appendix 1. Stable management	
"	8.10.15		Routine as yesterday. Lecture on Para II. & III.	
"	9.10.15		Lecture 9.30 am on Para III & IV. Pte Crabtree reported sick.	
"	10.10.15		Lecture on Para IV & V. Veterinary stores arrived and acknowledged. Mattresses 7 hours for AVS	
"	11.10.15		Garage 9.20 2½ hours dismounted drill. Lecture to all ranks on Appendix 1. Field dressing arrived	
"	12.10.15		Routine as yesterday. Horse destroyed belonging to No 231 60ASb. Arrangements made for inoculation. 14 men inoculated at 11 am with 1 dose 1 Agm 2nd Dose. Lecture 2.15 P.M. Appendix 11 & Para 1.	
"	13.10.15		Lecture to all ranks on Para 11 Appendix 1. Parade all ranks for Pay.	
"	14.10.15		Marching drill 2 hours. Cpl Gent. Admitted to Hospital. Invoice for case of Rifles received	
"	15.10.15		Camp routine as usual. Case of Rifles arrived from Ordnance	
"	16.10.15		Garage for 2½ hours foot drill. Mob: Stores drawn from Ordnance (Sections 1, 9a, 5a & 6)	
"	17.10.15			
"	18.10.15		2½ hours lecture on Appendix II Para III Standing Orders AVC. Leave granted to 1 Sgt & 10 men. Railway warrants issued	
"	19.10.15			

Army Form C. 2118.

WAR DIARY
or
INTELLIGENCE SUMMARY.
(Erase heading not required.)

Instructions regarding War Diaries and Intelligence Summaries are contained in F. S. Regs., Part II. and the Staff Manual respectively. Title pages will be prepared in manuscript.

28 MAY 1919
ROYAL ARMY VETY. CORPS.

Place	Date	Hour	Summary of Events and Information	Remarks and references to Appendices
WARMINSTER ENG	20.10.15		Parade for fitting Saddlery. Arrangement made with C.R.E. for instruction in Gas helmet drill	
"	21.10.15		Routine as usual. Cleaning and fitting Harness & Saddlery.	
"	22.10.15		Routine as yesterday	
"	23.10.15		Routine as usual. Attended lecture with section on use of Anti gas helmet. Pte Holmes sent to Remount Depot Salisbury to crew to Changes in orders from A.V.S.	
"	24.10.15		Fitting and making Harness & Saddlery.	
"	25.10.15		Kit Inspection for all ranks. Leave granted to remainder of Section, all other leave men reported base.	
"	26.10.15		Routine as usual. Two chargers mallined	
"	27.10.15		Men Inoculated 7 Dove. Corp Gent exchanged from Hospital stationery for Mobile Equipment owing Ammunition indented for for mobility. Mobilization Equipment arrived from France	
"	28.10.15		Routine as usual. Corp Gent granted 4 days leave	
"	29.10.15		Routine as usual. Indented for Horses (22) and saw D.A.D.A.S. as to their accommodation under Shelter.	
"	30.10.15		Routine as usual. Arrangement made for mobility.	
"	31.10.15		Routine as usual.	

M Liverney Major
for O.C.

WAR DIARY
or
INTELLIGENCE SUMMARY.
(Erase heading not required.)

Army Form C. 2118.

Instructions regarding War Diaries and Intelligence Summaries are contained in F. S. Regs., Part II. and the Staff Manual respectively. Title pages will be prepared in manuscript.

OFFICER-IN-CHARGE RECORDS
28 MAY 1919
ROYAL MILITARY VETY. CORPS.

Place	Date	Hour	Summary of Events and Information	Remarks and references to Appendices
WARMINSTER BKS.	1.11.15		Parade 9.30 am Rifles issued complete 9 to 11.45 Musketry Instruction. Col. Nugent's arrival visited section	
"	2.11.15		9 to 10.30 Musketry Instruction & Lecture on Aiming & arrangement in the field by Lt 12.03. Instruction on Musketry on Rifle range 9.20 10.30 & 4 Plats 5 Plats	
"	3.11.15		Aclong Parade for Rifle Instruction at Rifle range Accommodation for Horses Armoury work. A.D.3. 9. 6 R.E.	
"	4.11.15		Parade for Musketry Instruction Nothington Equipment around from Ordnance Pant of section (AP. 5 A)	
"	5.11.15			
"	6.11.15		Routine as yesterday Bandsmen issued to section	
"	7.11.15		Arranged with 1.5.0. to fire Musketry Course on Agway, on Range 6.	
"	8.11.15		Parades 4.15 am. and marched to Rifle range and completed Musketry course by firing Nos 3. 4 & 5. Part 1 & Nos 6. Part 2 Round at Range 1091 Average 43.6 per man of Instructional Cavalry. Return on Camp 12 appendices IV. Leewards to take change of Divisional Cavalry on arrival at Imman Dundle.	
"	9.11.15		Parade for Lecture on Fire & Appearance II Parade for Musketry Instruction issued	
"	10.11.15		Pte. Cooper started on course of Iced Shoeing Parade for Lecture on Pay & appendices II Lectures on Apparatus 1 & 2 Corps Alice & Cpl. Ellis rings around from Mountees Parade for rifle Inspection & recall Parade all hands for pay.	
"	11.11.15			
"	12.11.15			
"	13.11.15		Parade 9.30 am for 2½ hours rifle drill	
"	14.11.15		Lecture on yesterday Pte Robbins admitted to Hospital	
"	15.11.15		Parade 9.30 am & hour route march Lecture on Jetting Saddlery	
"	16.11.15		Rout march 9 am to 11.0 Pm. 15 am Practical Lecture on Jetting Saddlery	

Army Form C. 2118

WAR DIARY
or
INTELLIGENCE SUMMARY.
(Erase heading not required.)

Instructions regarding War Diaries and Intelligence Summaries are contained in F.S. Regs., Part II. and the Staff Manual respectively. Title pages will be prepared in manuscript.

OFFICER-IN-CHARGE RECORDS
26 MAY 1919
ROYAL ARMY VET. CORPS.

Place	Date	Hour	Summary of Events and Information	Remarks and references to Appendices
WARMINSTER ENG	17.11.15		9.15 to 10.15 am dismounted drill 2 Sgts vaccinated. Parade 2.15 PM for fittings harness & saddlery	
	18.11.15		Stables 6.30 am. Parade 9.30 am feeding given on practical way of feeding. Securing animals in open & Pickets to Paddocks	
	19.11.15		Routine as usual. Stables 6.30 to 8 am & 9.30 to 11.15 am. 2.15 PM to 3.15 PM Lectures on equipment & fitting of same.	
	20.11.15		Routine as usual. Pte Holmes sent to Woolwich veterinary stores issued to took sick horses	
	21.11.15		Routine as usual. Roving drill for seven men who had never ridden before	
	22.11.15		Routine as usual. 8.15 PM issued to 12 G.T. GOV men complete saddlery equipment No 10,1372 S.S. springer & No 1892 Pte M Dealer reported from Woolwich	
	23.11.15		Lecture on fitting harness, saddlery, 2 men vaccinated & men inoculated. Fee by GSO1 Woolwich section	
	24.11.15		Routine as usual. Gun section 2a. 2b chosen from remains 10 Sealed section to inspect men inoculated	
	25.11.15		Routine as usual. Prepare Lines for animals coming in next to section	
	26.11.15		Routine as usual 9 cases admitted Park of stores from Woolwich	
	26.11.15		Routine as usual 7 cases admitted Second Park of stores arrives	
	27.11.15		Routine as usual P.M letter in march 7.7.P.M.	
	28.11.15		Routine as usual Remonstration in case in stock won't special reference to stem cases with horsey stores assembly Mule try answer from Woolwich	
	29.11.15		Routine as usual 1 case admitted to Hospital Riding drill for 2 new G.S. Section Horses	
	30.11.15		Further Demonstration all cases flotting & use of counter irritants Special reference to Pneumonia cases	

M J McNamara
Capt
for

WAR DIARY
or
INTELLIGENCE SUMMARY.
(Erase heading not required.)

Army Form C. 2118.

OFFICER-IN-CHARGE RECORDS
28 MAY 1919

Instructions regarding War Diaries and Intelligence Summaries are contained in F. S. Regs., Part II. and the Staff Manual respectively. Title pages will be prepared in manuscript.

Place	Date	Hour	Summary of Events and Information	Remarks and references to Appendices
WARMINSTER ENG	1.12.15		Routine as usual. Lecture 9 to 11. To include all transport officers & men of section. 2 cases admitted. Vriefing gear drawn from Ordnance	
"	2.12.15		Routine as usual. Lecture same as yesterday. 1 Mule destroyed (Septic Villitis) Mallures 1 Horse belonging to North Irish Horse	
"	3.12.15		Routine as usual. 5 cases admitted	
"	4.12.15		Routine as usual. 1 Mule destroyed	
"	5.12.15		Routine as usual. 1 Horse destroyed. Fractures Tibia)	
"	6.12.15		Routine as usual. Lecture given to transport under studies	
"	7.12.15		Routine as usual. Lecture as previous. Arrangements made for sick animals to go to Veterinary Hospital Bulford. 4 cases admitted	
"	8.12.15		Routine as usual. Lecture as yesterday. 5 cases admitted	
"	9.12.15		Routine as usual. 6 cases transferred to S Veterinary Hospital Bulford. Pte Hall WD 4104 from Woolwich	
"	10.12.15		Routine as usual. Lecture to transport under studys. Arrangements made for sick animals to go to S.V.H. Bulford. 1 Horse taken on strength of Section from 176th Coy AF.A.	
"	11.12.15		Routine as usual. Lecture to transport under study. 7 cases sent to S.V.H. Bulford. 2 cases admitted. 7 Horses Mares (WD50)	
"	12.12.15		Routine as usual. Lecture as yesterday. 1 Horse admitted. Received orders to mobilize to take effect from 13.12.15 on General Scheme laid down by W.O.	
"	13.12.15		Routine as usual. 3 cases admitted. 17 cases transferred to S.V.H. Bulford. Jct Inspection checked mobilization stores. Lectured to J.O.s of Field Ambulance. Intended for Horse Shoes	
"	14.12.15		Routine as usual. 18 cases transferred to S.Vet.Hos. BULFORD	
"	15.12.15		Routine as usual. 1 Mule destroyed. 5 cases admitted	
"	16.12.15		Routine as usual. 24 cases admitted. Arrangements made to transfer sick animals to Vet Hos BULFORD	

WAR DIARY
or
INTELLIGENCE SUMMARY.
(Erase heading not required.)

Army Form. C. 2118.

OFFICER-IN-CHARGE
28 MAY 1919
ROYAL ARMY VETY. CORPS.

Instructions regarding War Diaries and Intelligence Summaries are contained in F. S. Regs., Part II. and the Staff Manual respectively. Title pages will be prepared in manuscript.

Place	Date	Hour	Summary of Events and Information	Remarks and references to Appendices
WARMINSTER	17.12.15		Routine as usual. 30 cases transferred sick to S.V.S. BULFORD 7 cases admitted	
"	18.12.15		Routine as usual. 21 cases admitted to Hosp. Arrangement made to transfer sick cases to-morrow.	
"	19.12.15		Routine as usual. Evacuation impossible no train service 1 Horse admitted. Waggons, saddles, Hay nets & plant to drawn from O'nance	
"	20.12.15		19 cases transferred sick to Veterinary Hospital BULFORD 9 cases admitted	
"	21.12.15		Routine as usual 6 cases admitted Arrangement made for evacuation of sick animals to-morrow.	
"	22.12.15		Routine as usual 18 cases transferred sick to Veterinary Hospital BULFORD. 1 Horse destroyed. Horse shoes drawn from O'nance	
"	23.12.15		Routine as usual 2 A.S.C. drivers reported for duty. 1 Mule destroyed 13 cases admitted	
"	24.12.15		14 cases arrived from A.V.C. for Section. Routine as usual 15.6 cases transferred sick to Veterinary Hosp BULFORD 11 cases admitted A.D.V.S. inspected Section Horses	
"	25.12.15		Routine as usual.	
"	26.12.15		Feeding drill for Section 9 to 11 am. 2 P.M Harness & Saddlery cleaning 1 case admitted	
"	27.12.15		Routine as usual 7 cases admitted Arrangement made for evacuation of sick animals tomorrow	
"	28.12.15		Routine as usual. 20 cases transferred sick to Veterinary Hospital BULFORD 8 cases admitted	
"	29.12.15		Routine as usual 10 cases admitted	
"	30.12.15		Routine as usual. 17 cases transferred sick to Veterinary Hospital BULFORD 17 cases admitted	
"	31.12.15		Routine as usual 6 cases admitted Arrangement made to transfer sick to-morrow 1 Mule destroyed. Horses clipped those trace high	

Wilkinson
Colt.

Confidential

War Diary

of

44th Mobile Veterinary Section
34th Division

from 7th January 1916 to 31st January 1916

(Volume 1)

Army Form C. 2118.

WAR DIARY
or
~~INTELLIGENCE SUMMARY.~~
(Erase heading not required.)

Instructions regarding War Diaries and Intelligence Summaries are contained in F.S. Regs., Part II and the Staff Manual respectively. Title pages will be prepared in manuscript.

Hour, Date, Place	Summary of Events and Information	Remarks and references to Appendices
Sutton Veny 7-1-16	Routine as usual. 10 a.m. Marching order parade mounted & Inspection. Surplus Equipment returned to Depot Woolwich. Mobilization equipment packed ready to put in limbers. 2.15 p.m. Parade for fray. WyB	
" 8-1-16.	Routine as usual. 9 a.m. Marching order parade & route march. Finished packing Mob: Stores in Wagons. Men cleaning up & disinfecting Hospital. WyB	
" 9-1-16	Routine as usual. Mounted parade & inspection. All Hut scrubbed out with Creosol & all Barrack stores checked ready to hand over to-morrow. WyB	
" 10-1-16.	6.30 Stables 7.15 a.m. Breakfast 11.30 Parade of Section & transport in marching order. Keys handed over to 2nd Lieut Sedgewick 11th Suffolks as O.C. Details & Barrack Stores checked in his presence. 12-15 p.m marched from Sutton Veny arrived Warminster Station 1-10 h.m & entrained horses & wagons. Left Warminster 3 h.m arrived Southampton 5-15 detrained & embarked on S.S. Machaeran. Left Southampton 6.45 p.m. WyB	

(73989) W4141—463. 400,000. 9/14. H.&J.Ltd. Forms/C. 2118/10.

Army Form C. 2118.

WAR DIARY
or
INTELLIGENCE SUMMARY.
(Erase heading not required.)

Instructions regarding War Diaries and Intelligence Summaries are contained in F. S. Regs., Part II and the Staff Manual respectively. Title pages will be prepared in manuscript.

Hour, Date, Place	Summary of Events and Information	Remarks and references to Appendices
On board S.S. Machinar 11/1/16.	Arrived Le Havre 6 a.m. & lay out in the "Roads" docked at 11.30 a.m. & disembarked, all clean at 3.30 p.m. Marched to No 1 Rest Camp, Havre arrived there 5-15. Horses watered, fed & all harness removed. Left Rest Camp 8 p.m. French Interpreter M. Lammier reported for duty. Marched to Point No 1 arrived 9.30 p.m. entrained & left Havre 12.10 a.m. (Cab covers, drivers coats drawn from Ordnance at Havre)	MB
In the Train 12-1-16.	In the train. Stopped at Abbeyville one hour for watering & feeding horses. Arrived St. Omer 5-40 p.m. detrained & marched for billets at 9 p.m. Guide incompetent & lost whole convoy, arrived billet at Eblinghem Station at 12.30 a.m. & picketed horses. No casualties in either men or horses on journey, the latter standing journey very well.	MB
Eblinghem 13-1-16.	Stables 7 a.m. Reported in person to A.D.V.S. at Headquarters & was ordered by him to find a more suitable billet nearer Bd. Hd. Qrs. Found suitable billet & accommodation to move. Rations drawn from No 2 Co. A.S.C. at Renescure	MB

(73989) W4141—463. 400,000. 9/14. H.&J.Ltd. Forms/C. 2118/10.

WAR DIARY
~~INTELLIGENCE SUMMARY~~
(Erase heading not required.)

Army Form C. 2118.

Instructions regarding War Diaries and Intelligence Summaries are contained in F.S. Regs., Part II. and the Staff Manual respectively. Title pages will be prepared in manuscript.

Hour, Date, Place		Summary of Events and Information	Remarks and references to Appendices
Ellelingham	14-1-16	Stables at 6.30 a.m. Parade 10 a.m. & moved Section to a farm ½ mile from Chateau & Nielle on Chateau & Nielle-la Grosse road. Reported arrival to A.D.V.S. & that Section was ready to receive & treat cases sent to it. Went to Renescure to arrange about forage for sick horses. 2 Horses admitted to Section. MyB	2 cases under treatment.
La Nieppe	15-1-16	Routine as usual. Cleaning up farm preparatory to receiving horses. Pass obtained from A.P.M. 3 patients admitted MyB	5 " "
"	16-1-16	Routine as usual. D.A.D.M.S. inspected billet & sanitary arrangements. A.D.V.S. inspected Section, informed me St Omer was Railhead & all cases to be evacuated to No 13 Veterinary Hospital. 4 cases admitted.	9 " "
"	17-1-16	Routine as usual. Went to St Omer & interviewed R.T.O & R.S.O. with regard to evacuating horses from Railhead. Opened an Imprest Account & drew 5 b fr. for payment of men. 4-15 h.m. Parade for hay. 16 cases admitted MyB	25 " "

WAR DIARY
or
~~INTELLIGENCE SUMMARY~~

(Erase heading not required.)

Army Form C. 2118.

Instructions regarding War Diaries and Intelligence Summaries are contained in F.S. Regs., Part II and the Staff Manual respectively. Title pages will be prepared in manuscript.

Hour, Date, Place	Summary of Events and Information	Remarks and references to Appendices
La Miche 17-1-16 (cont).	7 men & one horse of 49th Sanitary Section 3.4th Division attached to Section for Rations & billeting	
" 18-1-16.	Routine as usual. One horse destroyed (fracture of radius). Supply Wagon returned to No 1 Co. A.S.C. 14 cases admitted	38 cases under treatment.
" 19-1-16.	Routine as usual. Arrangements made to evacuate horses to - manoeuvre cases selected, 20 in all. Requisition Officer seen re obtaining hay to supplement present day ration of 6 lbs. 24 patients admitted	62 " " "
" 20-1-16.	20 cases "transferred Sick" from St-Omer as railroad to No 13 Veterinary Hospital, Neufchatel. N.C.O. i/c party Sgt. Owen. 2 Horses died. 8 horses admitted	48 " " "
" 21-1-16	Routine as usual. 9 a.m. Inspection of Rifles, gas helmets, iron rations etc. 4 horses returned to duty w/d units. 13 cases admitted. 25b tails of hay obtained by requisition. Billeting party sent to Hdqrs 26th Division & new billets allotted at Steenbecque.	59 " " "

Army Form C. 2118.

WAR DIARY
or
INTELLIGENCE SUMMARY.
(Erase heading not required.)

Instructions regarding War Diaries and Intelligence Summaries are contained in F. S. Regs., Part II. and the Staff Manual respectively. Title pages will be prepared in manuscript.

Hour, Date, Place	Summary of Events and Information	Remarks and references to Appendices
Le Pietre 22-1-16.	Routine as usual. 6 horses returned to duty with their units	68 cases under treatment
3-10 p.m.	Received orders that Division would move to-morrow. Times to be given later. Sgt. Owen & three men reported from Neufchatel (conducting party). Veterinary Service Labels & Horse evacuation rolls received from A.D.V.S. 17 cases admitted. WWB	
Le Pietre - 23-1-16.	Stables 6 a.m.	" 0 " "
9.30 a.m.	Parade moved off 10 a.m. from billet & proceeded with 64 sick horses & mules to Steenbecque via Reserune & Lynde. Arrived Steenbecque 2.20 p.m. & took over the billet lately occupied by the M.V.S. of 2nd Division. Reported in writing & in person to A.D.V.S at Blaringham. 3 miles of 46th Div. Train A.S.C admitted to Section Horse destroyed (fracture of pelvis) at Le Pietre. WWB	
Steenbecque 24-1-16.	Routine as usual. Cases further selected for evacuation to-morrow & arrangements made with R.T.O & R.S.O at Steenbecque Station	Y4 " "
	4 horses admitted including one from No 6 Reserve Park A.S.C. WWB	

Army Form C. 2118.

WAR DIARY
~~INTELLIGENCE SUMMARY~~
(Erase heading not required.)

Instructions regarding War Diaries and Intelligence Summaries are contained in F. S. Regs., Part II and the Staff Manual respectively. Title pages will be prepared in manuscript.

Hour, Date, Place	Summary of Events and Information	Remarks and references to Appendices
Steenbecque 25-1-16.	Routine as usual. 38 cases transferred sick to No 13 Veterinary Hospital. Sgt Rose & six men as conducting party. KMB 4 horses admitted to Hospital.	46 cases under treatment.
" 26-1-16.	Routine as usual. 4 horses returned to duty with units. One horse admitted to Section. Received orders, to collect two horses left by 2nd Division from A.W.V.S. MyB	37 "
" 27-1-16.	Routine as usual. 2 horses collected from Mde Q. Canten, Ferme le Hopital, Blaringhem left by 158 Co A.S.C. 20th Division, one pneumonia, one laminitis. MyB One horse returned to duty, cured. 3 horses admitted including above.	39 "
" 28-1-16.	Routine as usual. 5 horses returned to duty with units. One " admitted. Opened Imprest Account with field cashier at Blaringham & drew 1000 frs for payment of men. 2 h. am Inspection of rifles iron rations etc. 2.15 parade for hay. 3.40 h.am Orders from A.W.V.S to collect two horses at Wittes. MyB	35 "

WAR DIARY
or
~~INTELLIGENCE SUMMARY~~

(Erase heading not required.)

Army Form C. 2118.

Instructions regarding War Diaries and Intelligence Summaries are contained in F.S. Regs., Part II. and the Staff Manual respectively. Title pages will be prepared in manuscript.

Hour, Date, Place	Summary of Events and Information	Remarks and references to Appendices
Stombecque 29-1-16.	Routine as usual. 2 horses returned to units for duty. Two horses collected from M. le Moine, Witter left by 20th Div: A.F.A. 128 Brig". Received orders to collect one horse & two mules from Arques.	34 cases under treatment
" 30-1-16.	Routine as usual. One horse (25th N.F.) collected from M. Fernand Carlier Carlier, Arques, also one mule 34th D.A.C. One mule from M. Leon Carrier, Font Rouge Estaminet 34th D.A.C.	38 " " "
9-15am	No 8164 Pte Ramage J; H.L.I. 15th Division put under "close arrest" & sent under escort to 22nd Northumberland Fusiliers to be put in guard room for the night & sent to A.P.M in the morning. Charge = "Absent without leave." 4 horses admitted.	
" 31-1-16.	Routine as usual. A.D.V.S. inspected Section & ordered me to take over Veterinary charge of:– 1st Echelon 6th ~~Field~~ Base Reserve Park A.S.C., 1st Echelon 14th Reserve Park A.S.C & Headquarters 3rd Corps & attached units. Arrangements made to evacuate horses from Section to-morrow. 2 Horses admitted.	40 " " "

W. J. Bainbridge / Lieut
O.C. 1.4 M.V.S.
M.V.S.

34

44 ᵗʰ Moh: Veh: Sch:
vol: 2

CONFIDENTIAL

WAR DIARY

of

44th Mobile Veterinary Section

34th Division.

from 1st Feb 1916 to 29th Feb 1916.

(Volume 2.)

Army Form C. 2118.

WAR DIARY
or
INTELLIGENCE SUMMARY

(Erase heading not required.)

Instructions regarding War Diaries and Intelligence Summaries are contained in F. S. Regs., Part II. and the Staff Manual respectively. Title pages will be prepared in manuscript.

Hour, Date, Place	Summary of Events and Information	Remarks and references to Appendices
Steenbecque 1-2-16	Routine as usual. 24 cases transferred sick to No 13 Veterinary Hospital, including one mule cast by Remounts. 4 horses admitted #5 " " returned to units	13 cases under treatment.
" 2-2-16	Routine as usual. 3 cases admitted 2.15 p.m. parade for inspection of gas helmets respirators etc.	16 " " "
" 3-2-16	Routine as usual. Conducting party reported from Neufchatel. 9 cases admitted	25 " " "
" 4-2-16	Routine as usual. 4 horses admitted 3 cases returned to units	26 " " "
" 5-2-16	Routine as usual. 2 horses admitted. Arrangements made to evacuate Section to-morrow A.O.A.M.S. inspected billets	23 " " "
" 6-2-16	Routine as usual. 22 cases transferred sick to No 13 Hospital. 2 cases admitted	3 " " "

Army Form C. 2118.

WAR DIARY
or
~~INTELLIGENCE SUMMARY~~

(Erase heading not required.)

Instructions regarding War Diaries and Intelligence Summaries are contained in F.S. Regs., Part II and the Staff Manual respectively. Title pages will be prepared in manuscript.

Hour, Date, Place	Summary of Events and Information	Remarks and references to Appendices
Steenbecque 7-2-16.	Routine as usual. 12 horses admitted including 3 cast by Remounts.	20 cases under treatment
" 8-2-16	Routine as usual. 10 cases admitted. H/P	30 " " "
" 9-2-16	Routine as usual. 4 horses admitted. Arrangements made to transfer sick to-morrow. H/P	34 " " "
" 10-2-16	Routine as usual. 2.8 horses & mules transferred sick to No 13 Veterinary Hospital. 4 horses admitted. H/P	10 " " "
" 11-2-16.	Routine as usual. 100 francs drawn from Field Cashier on Imprest account. 2 horses admitted. H/P	12 " " "
" 12-2-16.	Routine as usual. A.D.V.S. 23rd Division inspected Section preparatory to 22nd Division taking over listed. 5 horses admitted. H/P	19 " " "
" 13-2-16.	Routine as usual. Horse died (pneumonia). 3 horses admitted. H/P	19 " " "
" 14-2-16.	Routine as usual. 8 horses admitted. Arrangements made to evacuate to-morrow. H/P	24 " " "

WAR DIARY
or
INTELLIGENCE SUMMARY

(Erase heading not required.)

Army Form C. 2118.

Instructions regarding War Diaries and Intelligence Summaries are contained in F.S. Regs., Part II and the Staff Manual respectively. Title pages will be prepared in manuscript.

Hour, Date, Place	Summary of Events and Information	Remarks and references to Appendices
Steenwerque 15-2-16	Routine as usual. 22 horses "transferred sick" to No 13 hospital including 3 cast by Remounts. 4 horses admitted. Received orders to march to Steenwerque Area on 18-2-16. MyB	9 Cases under treatment.
16-2-16	Routine as usual. One horse admitted MyB	10 " " "
17-2-16	Routine as usual. One horse admitted. Preparation made to move to-morrow. MyB	11 " " "
18-2-16	Marched from billet at 9.30 a.m. & proceeded with Section to billet in Steenwerk Area lately vacated by M.V.S of 23rd Division at H.1.b.6.8. (Sheet 36). Returned animal by wire to 34th Division & in hansen to A.V.V.S, 23rd Division. 7 horses taken over by from 23rd Division. Billet very dirty & uninviting. MyB	18 " " "
Croix-du-Bac 19-2-16	No 4527 Cpl Gwilt J.R. despatched to Vieux-les Mines as evidence at court martial of 15th Division re desertion of Pte Ramage 15th H.L.I. Parade for hay 2.30 p.m. Direct found at Steenwerck & A.V.V.S wires to that effect. 3 horses admitted. MyB	21 " " "

WAR DIARY
or
~~INTELLIGENCE SUMMARY~~

(Erase heading not required.)

Army Form C. 2118.

Hour, Date, Place	Summary of Events and Information	Remarks and references to Appendices
Croix-du-Bac. 20.2.16.	Routine as usual. Wire from A.D.V.S. instructing one to evacuate new billet. Marched from billet 2.40 h.m. to Steenwerck & occupied new billet at A.23.6.2.b. (Sheet 36). Horses destroyed (Tetanus) 2 horses.	20 cases under treatment.
Steenwerck 21.2.16	Routine as usual. One horse collected, left leg 23". D division at River Bradbury. 2 horses admitted. Cpl. Gent returned from 15th D Division. Arrangements made to evacuate section to ------	22 " "
" 22.2.16	Routine as usual. 16 horses "transferred sick" 6 No 13 Hospital. 9.50 h.m. received telegram from A.P.M. 1st D Division for No 4527 Cpl Gent S.R. to report again on Thursday No 4559 Privates - horses for F.G.C.M. as evidence 24.2.16 at Hurdles. One horse returned to duty. 3 horses admitted.	8 " "
" 23.2.16.	Routine as usual. Cpl. Gent despatched to ------ horses. 2 horses returned to duty. 5 admitted.	11 " "

Army Form C. 2118.

WAR DIARY
or
INTELLIGENCE SUMMARY

(Erase heading not required.)

Instructions regarding War Diaries and Intelligence Summaries are contained in F.S. Regs., Part II and the Staff Manual respectively. Title pages will be prepared in manuscript.

Hour, Date, Place	Summary of Events and Information	Remarks and references to Appendices
Steenwerck 24-2-16.	Routine as usual. No 892 Cpl. Hunting H.H. charged by A.P.M. 2nd Division with entering an estaminet while on duty. Placed under arrest. 3 horses admitted, one returned to duty.	13 cases under treatment
25-2-16.	Routine as usual. A.D.V.S. inspected Section.	20 "
2.15pm Parade for kray & inspection of all kit. 4 horses admitted. Sgt Rose F. No 1271 reported sick & excused duty 3 days		
	Arrangements made to evacuate Section to-morrow.	
26.2.16.	No 892 Cpl: Hunting H.H. brought to Orderly Room & sentenced to "Reprimand" awarded. Ch. Gent reported from Pouvus Lu Mines. 16 horses admitted. Mule shot & one horse destroyed	28 "
27.2.16.	Routine as usual. 24 horses Transferred Sick to No 13 Idstable including 3 cast by Destroyed. One horse admitted	2 "
28-2-16.	Routine as usual. 10 cases admitted	19 "

Army Form C. 2118.

WAR DIARY
or
INTELLIGENCE SUMMARY
(Erase heading not required.)

Instructions regarding War Diaries and Intelligence Summaries are contained in F.S. Regs., Part II. and the Staff Manual respectively. Title pages will be prepared in manuscript.

Hour, Date, Place	Summary of Events and Information	Remarks and references to Appendices
Steenwerck 29-2-16.	Routine as usual. D.D.V.S. 1st Army inspected Section & gave a demonstration on lecture on the Intra Dermal Ocular Palpebral test for Glanders. 2 horses admitted	14 cases under treatment.

W.J. Bainbridge / Lieut
O.C. 44th Mobile Veterinary Section.

CONFIDENTIAL

WAR DIARY

of

44ᵗʰ MOBILE VETERINARY SECTION.

from 1ˢᵗ March 1916 to 31ˢᵗ March 1916.

(Volume 3)

WAR DIARY
or
INTELLIGENCE SUMMARY

Army Form C. 2118.

(Erase heading not required.)

Instructions regarding War Diaries and Intelligence Summaries are contained in F.S. Regs., Part II. and the Staff Manual respectively. Title pages will be prepared in manuscript.

Hour, Date, Place	Summary of Events and Information	Remarks and references to Appendices
Steenwerck 1st March 1916.	Routine as usual. Horses admitted one. 15 men sent to Erquingham for Baths at 104 Field Ambulance. MWB	
2nd " "	Horses admitted 13. Arrangements made to evacuate sick horses to-morrow. MWB	
3rd " "	32 cases transferred sick to No 13 Veterinary Hospital. Mule destroyed (septic leg) from 209 Field Co R.E. No 872 Cpl Hunting H. returned sick & admitted to Hospital of 103rd Field Amb. (distended feet). three one horses admitted. MWB	
4th " "	Routine as usual, one horse admitted. MWB	
5th " "	one Sgt & 4 men sent to 2nd Div. at Boeslen, under orders from G.O.C. R.m.G., 34th Div., to fetch 9 H.D. remounts. No 1349 Pte Hale F.R. returned sick & admitted to Hospital. 3 Horses admitted. MWB	
6th " "	4 Horses admitted. No 11892 Pte Dexter Gn appointed Acting Corporal. only one N.C.O. is left with Section. MWB	

Army Form C. 2118.

WAR DIARY
or
~~INTELLIGENCE SUMMARY~~
(Erase heading not required.)

Instructions regarding War Diaries and Intelligence Summaries are contained in F.S. Regs., Part II and the Staff Manual respectively. Title pages will be prepared in manuscript.

Hour, Date, Place	Summary of Events and Information	Remarks and references to Appendices
Steenwerck 7th March 1916.	Sgt. Owen reported back from 2nd Division with 9 H.R. remounts. R.A.Q.M.G. advised & orders issued to supply units on demand. One horse admitted. MpB	
8th " "	Remounts issued & receipts for same forwarded to D.A.Q.M.G. Horse admitted from 3th Div: Cavalry for Mallein test. Inoculated by English & French method 2.15 p.m. 7 Horses admitted. MpB	
9th " "	Routine as usual. No reaction from above horse. 2 horses admitted. Rifle & kit inspection. MpB	
10th " "	Horse from No. 3 Coy. A.S.C. admitted for mallein test. Injected by French & English method 2.45 p.m. Arrangements made to evacuate sick horses to-morrow. 4 cases admitted. MpB	
11th " "	26 horses transferred sick to No 13 Hospital. A.S.C. horse tested yesterday suspicious reaction in Off eye. No reaction in sick & no temperature. A.R.V.S. informed &, visited Section & examined horse. MpB	
12th " "	No 8 & 2 Pl. Hunting H.H. returned to duty from hospital. 4 horses admitted. MpB	

WAR DIARY
or
INTELLIGENCE SUMMARY

(Erase heading not required.)

Army Form C. 2118.

Instructions regarding War Diaries and Intelligence Summaries are contained in F.S. Regs., Part II and the Staff Manual respectively. Title pages will be prepared in manuscript.

Hour, Date, Place	Summary of Events and Information	Remarks and references to Appendices
Steenwerck 13th March 1916.	Routine as usual. Rifle & bit inspection. 5 horses admitted	
" 14th "	Horse admitted from 152nd Brig. Amm. Coll. R.F.A. for mallein test. Injected in neck & off eye 5.30 p.m. 3 horses admitted. A.S.C. junction.	WB
" 15th "	Horse admitted yesterday reacted to test bad. in eye & neck especially in former. Arrangements made to evacuate to morrow. A.D.V.S. inspected Section & examined horse reacting to test.	WB
" 16th "	Horse admitted from 152nd Brig. Amm. Coll. for testing, injected 8.30 a.m. 7 other cases admitted. D.D.V.S. 1st Army visited Section, examined reacting horse & inspected Section, ordered horse to be destroyed & P.M. examination to be made. 2.5 cases transferred sick to No 13 hospital. 2 horses admitted.	WB
" 17th "	Horse from 152nd Brig. Amm. Coll. + all D.O.s of Division. Glanders nodule found in lung & when on nasal septum. Report forwarded to D.D.V.S. 8 cases admitted. Rifle & bit inspection.	WB

(73989) W4141—463. 400,000. 9/14. H.&J.Ltd. Forms/C. 2118/10.

Army Form C. 2118.

WAR DIARY
or
INTELLIGENCE SUMMARY.
(Erase heading not required.)

Instructions regarding War Diaries and Intelligence Summaries are contained in F. S. Regs., Part II. and the Staff Manual respectively. Title pages will be prepared in manuscript.

Hour, Date, Place	Summary of Events and Information	Remarks and references to Appendices
Steenwerck 18th March 1916.	Routine as usual. 4 horses admitted. Col: Hunting reported from No 13 Hospital. HyB	
" 19th "	Horse destroyed No 1 Coy A.S.C (Septic hock) Parade & inspection of all rifles, kit, etc. HyB 2 horses admitted	
" 20th "	Arrangements made to evacuate to-morrow to No 13 Hospital. 7 cases admitted. HyB	
" 21st "	21 cases transferred Sick to No 13 Hospital, 12 of these belonging to 39th Division. 3 horses admitted. HyB	
" 22nd "	Routine as usual. One horse returned to duty 8 horses admitted. HyB	
" 23rd "	One horse returned to duty. 8 horses admitted. HyB	
" 24th "	Horse from No 4 Coy. A.S.C destroyed Septic leg. A.D.V.S, 2nd Army visited Section 2 p.m. 34th Div. has to-day been transferred from 3rd Corps, 1st Army to 2nd Corps, 2nd Army. 4 horses admitted. HyB	

WAR DIARY
or
INTELLIGENCE SUMMARY.
(Erase heading not required.)

Army Form C. 2118.

Hour, Date, Place	Summary of Events and Information	Remarks and references to Appendices
Steenwerck 25th March 1916.	Arrangements made to evacuate sick horses to manoeuvre. No 4690 Pte Richardson P.C. returned for duty from No 1 Veterinary Hospital to replace No 13490 Pte Hall E.R. MyB	
" 26th "	22 horses transferred sick including two mares in foal. Horse from 152nd Brig: AmmCol & No 3 Coy A.S.C. again tested with malein. Lost in eye & neck. Inspection of rifles etc P.H. anti-gas helmets issued to all ranks to replace obsolete ones. 600 anti gas helmets (horse) drawn from ordnance No 10150 Pte Cooper H.J. admitted to Hospital suffering from measles. Billet sprayed with creosote & blankets disinfected. Horses admitted. 4. MyB	
" 27th "	360 Anti gas helmets Horse issued to D.A.C. & those horses tested yesterday of 152nd Brig: R.F.A., a slight swelling of lower lid only. 5 men sent to Divisional Baths. Horses admitted 8 MyB	
" 28th "	Routine as usual. 5 men sent to Divisional Baths. 4 horses admitted. MyB	
" 29th "	Routine as usual. 5 horses admitted. 5 men sent to Divisional Baths. MyB	

Army Form C. 2118.

WAR DIARY
or
INTELLIGENCE SUMMARY
(Erase heading not required.)

Instructions regarding War Diaries and Intelligence
Summaries are contained in F.S. Regs., Part II
and the Staff Manual respectively. Title pages
will be prepared in manuscript.

Hour, Date, Place	Summary of Events and Information	Remarks and references to Appendices
Steenwerck 30th March 1914.	Routine as usual. Inspection of all kit rifles etc. Arrangements made to evacuate to-morrow. 5 men sent to Divisional Baths. 2 horses admitted. WB	
31" "	18 cases transferred sick to No 13 Veterinary Hospital. 2 Horses collected from Mr Leon Gilléon, Steenwerck, left by 39th Division. Horse destroyed fractured pastern (charger) issued to Col Stephens 175 RFA WB Parade for hay. two horses admitted WB	

W. Bainbridge / Lieut
O.C. A.A. M.V.S.

Confidential

War Dairy

of

44th Mobile Veterinary Section.

34th Division.

(Volume 4).

From 1st April 1916. to 30th April 1916.

Army Form C. 2118.

WAR DIARY
or
INTELLIGENCE SUMMARY

(Erase heading not required.)

Instructions regarding War Diaries and Intelligence Summaries are contained in F.S. Regs., Part II and the Staff Manual respectively. Title pages will be prepared in manuscript.

Hour, Date, Place	Summary of Events and Information	Remarks and references to Appendices
Steenwerck 1st April 1916	Routine as usual. Inspection of rifles, helmets, saddlery etc. 2.1.15. 2 horses admitted.	
" 2nd "	Routine as usual. 2 horses destroyed. 4 admitted, one returned to duty.	
" 3rd "	Routine as usual. Hypodermic syringes & 220 doses of Mallein returned to P.D.V.S. 1st Army. Arrangements made to evacuate sick horses to-morrow. 13 horses admitted.	
" 4th "	28 cases transferred sick to No 13 Hospital including 2 cast leg remounts. One horse returned to Unit. 13 admitted.	
" 5th "	No 9764 Pte Higgins J. reported sick & admitted to Hospital. 4 horses admitted.	
" 6th "	Routine as usual. Cpl. Hunting K.H. reported unit conducting party minus No 6676 Pte Smith H.G. left under arrest at Neufchatel (drunk while on duty). 8 cases admitted.	
" 7th "	Routine as usual. Arrangements made to evacuate to-morrow. 29 cases admitted.	
" 8th "	40 cases transferred sick to No 13 Hospital. Received orders from A.D.V.S. that Section would move on 11-4-16. One horse admitted.	

Army Form C. 2118.

WAR DIARY
or
INTELLIGENCE SUMMARY.
(Erase heading not required.)

Instructions regarding War Diaries and Intelligence Summaries are contained in F. S. Regs., Part II. and the Staff Manual respectively. Title pages will be prepared in manuscript.

Hour, Date, Place	Summary of Events and Information	Remarks and references to Appendices
Steenwerck 9th April 1916	Telegram sent to O.C. No 13 Hospital asking for Pte Smith to be returned under escort of Sgt. in charge of conducting party. 6 orders received from Headquarters to move on 11-4-16 & proceed to Steenbecque stay there the night & march next day to Gilgues. 4 Horses admitted.	
10th " 1916.	2nd Australian Mobile Veterinary Section moved in to Billet 4 look over from this Section. all arrangements made to move to-morrow.	
11th " "	Reveille 3.45 a.m. Parade 6 a.m. & moved off from Steenwerck. 9 cases handed over to Australian M.V.S. Arrived Steenbecque 12-30 p.m. & Rations drawn from M.T. at Morbecque	
12th " "	Reveille 5 a.m. Parade 9.15 a.m. & moved off from Billet. One hour halt at Sr. O men midday feed, arrived Gilgues 1.30 p.m. Got into billet 5 p.m. Reported in person at Headquarters.	
13th " "	Routine as usual.	
14th " "	Routine as usual. Medical inspection all ranks 10 a.m.	

Army Form C. 2118.

WAR DIARY
or
INTELLIGENCE SUMMARY.
(Erase heading not required.)

Instructions regarding War Diaries and Intelligence Summaries are contained in F.S. Regs., Part II. and the Staff Manual respectively. Title pages will be prepared in manuscript.

Hour, Date, Place	Summary of Events and Information	Remarks and references to Appendices
Steenwerck Jilguis 15-4-16	Routine as usual. 6 Horses admitted.	
" 16-4-16	No 1040 Pte Power I awarded 5 days "confinent to Camp" for insolence to an N.C.O. 5 cases admitted	
" 17-4-16	Routine as usual. 4 Horses admitted.	
" 18-4-16	Routine as usual. D.A.V.S. inspected Section. No 14 73 Pte Hunt S. reported from No 13 Hospital for duty. Received orders to send G.S. limbered wagon to Abbeyville & draw Horse Ambulance in lieu. D.D.V.S cancelled order. 4 horses admitted. Inspection of rifles etc. Men from 19.5 ᵗʰ Brig. R.F.A. foaled.	
" 19-4-16.	Wire Telegram from D.D.V.S to send wagon to Abbeyville. 10 horses admitted. Arrangements made to evacuate 6 mannow.	
" 20-4-16.	Cpl Gent despatched to Abbeyville in charge of limbered wagon (3 days supplies) 27 cases transferred Sick from Water Station. 3 horses admitted.	
" 21-4-16.	Routine as usual. one horse admitted.	
" 22-4-16	Routine as usual. 2 cases admitted	

Army Form C. 2118.

WAR DIARY
or
INTELLIGENCE SUMMARY

(Erase heading not required.)

Instructions regarding War Diaries and Intelligence Summaries are contained in F.S. Regs., Part II and the Staff Manual respectively. Title pages will be prepared in manuscript.

Hour, Date, Place	Summary of Events and Information	Remarks and references to Appendices
Hilgues 23rd April 1916.	Routine as usual.	
" 24 " 1916.	Routine as usual. Parade for inspection of rifles etc. Received order 9-15 h.m to fetch 40 remounts from Watten Station to-morrow at 6-30 a.m.	
" 25th "	40 Remounts fetched from Watten Station & handed over to Royal Artillery. 3 horses admitted	
" 26th "	C/o. Sgt reported from Abbeyville with Horse Ambulance. Arrangements made to evacuate to-morrow. 3 cases admitted.	
" 27th "	20 Cases transferred Sick from Watten Station including 1 man & foal. One horse admitted.	
" 28th "	Routine as usual. 5 cases admitted.	
" 29th "	Routine as usual. 3 cases admitted	
" 30th "	Horse collected from Renescure (Louis Iroront) by Beast left by 18th Royal Hussars. 3 horses admitted.	

W.J. Bainbridge
O.C. 44 M.V.S.
/Capt

Army Form C. 2118.

WAR DIARY
or
INTELLIGENCE SUMMARY.

(Erase heading not required.)

Instructions regarding War Diaries and Intelligence Summaries are contained in F. S. Regs., Part II. and the Staff Manual respectively. Title pages will be prepared in manuscript.

Hour, Date, Place	Summary of Events and Information	Remarks and references to Appendices

(73989) W4141—463. 400,000. 9/14. H.&J.Ltd. Forms/C. 2118/10.

CONFIDENTIAL.

WAR DAIRY

of

44th MOBILE VETERINARY SECTION

34th DIVISION.

FROM 1st May 1916 TO 31st May 1916.

(Volume 5.)

Army Form C. 2118.

WAR DIARY
or
INTELLIGENCE SUMMARY.
(Erase heading not required.)

Instructions regarding War Diaries and Intelligence Summaries are contained in F.S.Regs., Part II. and the Staff Manual respectively. Title pages will be prepared in manuscript.

Hour, Date, Place	Summary of Events and Information	Remarks and references to Appendices
TILQUES May 1st 1916	Routine as usual. Shot sent to Hdqurs 21st H.F. to collect horse. Two horses admitted to Hospital. WMB	
" 2nd "	Routine as usual. 13 horses admitted. Arrangements made to evacuate to-morrow. WMB	
" 3rd "	18 horses 7 mules transferred sick to No 13 Veterinary Hospital including two float cases. 3 horses admitted. WMB	
" 4th "	Routine as usual. Received orders to move on 6th inst. WMB	
" 5th "	Routine as usual. Received orders 2.41 p.m entraining at St. Omer 2.41 p.m. All arrangements made to move to-morrow. No 11814 Pte J.A Frank brought to Orderly Room — changed mind attempted arrival on H.C.O. remanded for 6 days confined to move. WMB	
" 6th "	Marching order parade 10.30 a.m. + moved off from Billet, marched to St. Omer station, entrained 1 P.M & left at 2.41 P.M. WMB	
LONGNEAU " 7th "	Arrived Longneau 4.30 a.m. detrained & marched to BRESLE arrived June 12.15 & occupied billet. WMB	
BRESLE " 8th "	Received orders to change billets to-morrow moving to BEHENCOURT arrangements made accordingly. 2 horses admitted. WMB	

Army Form C. 2118.

WAR DIARY
or
~~INTELLIGENCE SUMMARY.~~
(Erase heading not required.)

Instructions regarding War Diaries and Intelligence Summaries are contained in F.S. Regs., Part II and the Staff Manual respectively. Title pages will be prepared in manuscript.

Hour, Date, Place		Summary of Events and Information	Remarks and references to Appendices
BRESLE	9th May 1916.	Moved off from BRESLE 10.30 a.m. & arrived BEHENCOURT 12.15 p.m. WMB	
BEHENCOURT	10"	Routine as usual. Cleaning up billets, 2 cases admitted. WMB	
"	11"	Routine as usual. A.D.V.S. inspected Section & informed me that sick horses were to be transferred Sick to No 22 Veterinary Hospital ABBEYVILLE. No 11814 Pte Frank J.A. tried by G.T.V.S. & awarded "Admonished". WMB	
"	12"	Routine as usual. WMB	
"	13"	Shrayer received as gift from R.S.P.C.A & acknowledged. One horse admitted. WMB	
"	14"	Routine as usual. 3 cases admitted. Rifles, dixies etc inspected. WMB	
"	15"	Routine as usual. WMB	
"	16"	Routine as usual. 6 horses admitted. WMB	
"	17"	Arrangements made with R.T.O at MERICOURT to evacuate to No 22 Veterinary Hospital to-morrow. 14 cases admitted. WMB	
"	18"	24 Cases transferred Sick to No 22 Veterinary Hospital. 3 cases admitted. WMB	

WAR DIARY
or
INTELLIGENCE SUMMARY

Army Form C. 2118.

(Erase heading not required.)

Instructions regarding War Diaries and Intelligence Summaries are contained in F.S. Regs., Part II. and the Staff Manual respectively. Title pages will be prepared in manuscript.

Hour, Date, Place	Summary of Events and Information	Remarks and references to Appendices
BEHENCOURT 19th May 1916	Routine as usual. Sgt. Rose proceeded on leave to England. 16 men sent to BRESLE for baths. 5 cases admitted. YMB	
20th "	Routine as usual. 5 horses from A.P.M. admitted, found straying on the roads. One sick horse admitted. Inspection of rifles, diaries etc. YMB	
21st "	Routine as usual. One admitted. YMB	
22nd "	Arrangements made to evacuate tomorrow 35 horses admitted also 4 from A.P.M. YMB	
23rd "	38 cases trans. Sick to No 22 Veterinary Hospital. 9 cases admitted. YMB	
24th "	Routine as usual. Cpl Gent sent to BERNAYCOURT for 2 chargers to be branded and sent to 101st Ind: Brig: 5 horses admitted. YMB	
25th "	Routine as usual. Inspection of rifles etc. 3 cases admitted. One horse returned to duty cured. YMB	
26th "	Routine as usual, one horse returned to duty. Arrangements made to evacuate tomorrow. YMB	
27th "	18 cases transferred sick to No 22 Veterinary Hospital two horses returned to duty, 2 admitted. Sgt. Rose reported from leave. YMB	
28th "	Routine as usual. One admitted. YMB	

WAR DIARY
or
INTELLIGENCE SUMMARY.
(Erase heading not required.)

Army Form C. 2118.

Hour, Date, Place	Summary of Events and Information	Remarks and references to Appendices
BEHENCOURT. 29th May 1916.	Routine as usual, 12 cases admitted, one returned. WyB	
" 30 " "	Arrangements made to evacuate to-morrow, 2 cases admitted, one returned to duty. Sarcoptic parasite found on horse admitted 29th. met from 146th Bdg. R.F.A. WyB	
" 31 " "	15 cases transferred sick to No 22 Veterinary Hospital. Handed over charge of Section to Lieut T.H.R. Elliot A.V.C. acting for me while on leave. WyB	

44th Mobile Veterinary
Section.

W.J.Bainbridge/
O.C. 44 M.V.S. Capt

CONFIDENTIAL

WAR DIARY

OF

44th MOBILE VETERINARY SECTION
34th DIVISION.

FROM 1st 6-16 TO 30th 6-16.

Volume 6.

34/ 44 MVS vol 6
JUNE

WAR DIARY
or
INTELLIGENCE SUMMARY.
(Erase heading not required.)

Army Form C. 2118.

Hour, Date, Place	Summary of Events and Information	Remarks and references to Appendices
BEHENCOURT 1st June 1916	Two horses of Section drowned at Mericourt Station while waiting for conducting party. 1 horse admitted. WB	
" 2nd " "	Float sent to D battery 116th Brigade, came N.Y. also sent to 102nd Infantry Brigade. Two dead horses removed from Mericourt station to Briele. 4 horses admitted. WB	
" 3rd " "	Inspection of rifles, area CC. 8 horses admitted. WB	
" 4th " "	Court of Enquiry held on drowning of two Section horses, 6 witnesses examined. 4 horses admitted. WB	
" 5th " "	Board held on iron Rations. 20 unserviceable. Shot dog bitten by a rabid dog. 7 horses admitted. WB	
" 6th " "	42 Remounts distance at Fichencourt Station taken to Section for issue. 39 handed over. Arrangements made to evacuate tomorrows. 1 horse admitted. WB	

Army Form C. 2118.

WAR DIARY
or
INTELLIGENCE SUMMARY.
(Erase heading not required.)

Hour, Date, Place	Summary of Events and Information	Remarks and references to Appendices
BEHENCOURT		
7th June 1916.	15 horses 1 mule transferred S.C.R. to No 22 Vety Hospital. WB	
8th " "	Routine as usual. WB	
9th " "	Routine as usual. 9 horses admitted. WB	
10th " "	4 horses banished. Inspection of rifles etc. Sgt Roe admitted to Hospital 102nd Field Ambulance Hamilies. WB	
11th " "	Routine as usual. 1 horse admitted. WB	
12th " "	A.D.V.S Inspected. Action Routine as usual. WB 1 horse admitted. WB	
13th " "	Arrangements made to evacuate casualties. 3 horses admitted. WB	

WAR DIARY
or
INTELLIGENCE SUMMARY.
(Erase heading not required.)

Army Form C. 2118.

Hour, Date, Place	Summary of Events and Information	Remarks and references to Appendices
BEHENCOURT 14th June 1916	19 horses transferred sick to No 7 Veterinary Hospital FORGES LES EAUX. 2 horses admitted. WB	
15th " "	Routine as usual. 1 horse admitted. WB	
16th " "	Reconnaissance ride partly to Becourt wood to survey horse killed by shell fire. 8 horses admitted. WB	
17th " "	Parade whole section 7.30. Proceeded by track to Ribemont to show route to be taken during operations, site of advanced dressing post. Sgt Owen & 12 men sent home. Proceeded with one man & N.C.O. to Becourt wood. Found horse already buried. 4 horses admitted. WB	
18th " "	Float sent to 76th at Dernancourt & also to Querrieu for a P.M. Arrangements made to evacuate demortous. Captains D.L.O. horse fired & 21st March No: Pony & General Unack's horse blistered. 4 horses admitted. WB	

Army Form C. 2118.

WAR DIARY
or
INTELLIGENCE SUMMARY.
(Erase heading not required.)

Instructions regarding War Diaries and Intelligence Summaries are contained in F.S. Regs., Part II. and the Staff Manual respectively. Title pages will be prepared in manuscript.

Hour, Date, Place	Summary of Events and Information	Remarks and references to Appendices
BEHENCOURT 19 June 1916	Routine as usual. 1 horse admitted. YWB	
" 20th " "	Inspection of rifles etc. Routine as usual. Reconnoitred new route. 11 horses admitted. YWB	
" 21st " "	Routine as usual. 4 horses admitted. YWB	
" 22nd " "	Received orders to move tomorrow. Arrangements made to move tomorrow. Arrangements made to evacuate from Mericourt. 7 horses admitted. YWB	
" 23rd " "	Parade 8.30 am. Moved off from Billet to new one at D 21.C. near A.S.C. train bivouacking. Orders to them past to-morrow. 2/2 horses sent to the 7 Veterinary Hospital. Reported to D.H.Q. 1 horse admitted. YWB	

WAR DIARY
INTELLIGENCE SUMMARY.
(Erase heading not required.)

Army Form C. 2118.

Hour, Date, Place	Summary of Events and Information	Remarks and references to Appendices
RIBEMONT. 24th June 1916.	Collecting post opened at E.20.a. at DERNANCOURT Cemetery. 1 Cpl. and 3 men left.	
25th " "	Sgt Proctor, No 534 reported for duty from the 23rd Fd Amb. Routine as usual. Horses at post. 7 horses admitted.	
26th " "	Routine as usual. 9 horses admitted post.	
27th " "	Routine as usual. Arrangements made to evacuate from others. At post. 7 horses 7 horses admitted	
28th " "	22 Remounts collected from Mericourt station & taken back to Section. 18 horses transferred over, 5 at post 6 horses admitted.	
29th " "	18 Remounts issued to Division. 5 horses admitted.	
30th " "	4 Remounts delivered to Infantry Brigade. Arrangements made to evacuate tomorrow. At post, 7 horses 11 horses admitted.	

34/ 44th MVS Vol 7

CONFIDENTIAL.

WAR DIARY
OF
44th MOBILE VETERINARY SECTION 34th DIVISION

From 1st July-16 to 31st July 16

Volume 7.

Army Form C. 2118.

WAR DIARY
or
INTELLIGENCE SUMMARY.
(Erase heading not required.)

Instructions regarding War Diaries and Intelligence Summaries are contained in F.S. Regs., Part II. and the Staff Manual respectively. Title pages will be prepared in manuscript.

Hour, Date, Place	Summary of Events and Information	Remarks and references to Appendices
RIBEMONT		
1st July 1916.	32 cases transferred sick. At post. Horses 19 Horses admitted WB	
2nd July 1916.	Routine as usual. No 87295 Pte Groom J. reported for duty. 9 Horses admitted. WB	
3rd " "	Arrangements made to evacuate tomorrow. Pte Holmes admitted to Hospital suffering from strain accident, caught between buffers. 7 Horses admitted WB	
4th " "	19 cases transferred sick to No 7 Veterinary Hospital. Pte Holmes transferred sick 3 Horses admitted WB	
BRESLE 5th July 1916	Moved from Bivouac next to BRESLE Bivouacking there. Handed over to 35th M.V.S. 23rd Division. WB 2 Horses admitted	
" 6th July 1916	Closed attending post, occupied by 35th M.V.S. 2 Horses admitted WB	

Army Form C. 2118.

WAR DIARY
OF
INTELLIGENCE SUMMARY.
(Erase heading not required.)

Instructions regarding War Diaries and Intelligence Summaries are contained in F.S. Regs., Part II. and the Staff Manual respectively. Title pages will be prepared in manuscript.

Hour, Date, Place	Summary of Events and Information	Remarks and references to Appendices
BRESLE		
7th July 1916	Routine as usual. 4 horses admitted. WB	
8th " "	Cpl Slater reported sick. WB	
9th " "	Cpl Dexter admitted to 10 2nd Field Ambulance at Franvillers. WB 12 Horses admitted.	
10th " "	8 Horses admitted. WB	
11th " "	Sgt Haslewood sent to No 2 Veterinary Hospital. Have 1000 francs from Field Cashier. Horse destroyed. WB	
12th " "	Routine as usual. 4 horses admitted. WB	
13th " "	4 horses admitted from 1st Division. WB 17 horses admitted.	

Army Form C. 2118.

WAR DIARY
or
INTELLIGENCE SUMMARY.
(Erase heading not required.)

Instructions regarding War Diaries and Intelligence Summaries are contained in F.S. Regs., Part II. and the Staff Manual respectively. Title pages will be prepared in manuscript.

Hour, Date, Place	Summary of Events and Information	Remarks and references to Appendices
BRESLE		
14th July 1916	Arrangements made to evacuate tomatoes. S.S. nipnights mare changed for Black horse of colonel 9th S.b Staffords. 12 horses admitted.	WJB
15th July 1916	23 cases transferred sick to No.7 Veterinary Hospital. Inspection of rifles etc. taken. 6 horses admitted.	WJB
16th " "	9 horses from 25th Bgde R.F.A. taken to Queren to Remount depot. 4 horses admitted.	WJB
17th " "	9 Animals (Remounts) collected from FRECHENCOURT station for the division. 5 horses admitted.	WJB
18th " "	Remounts issued. Arrangements to evacuate tomatoes. 7 horses admitted.	WJB
19th " "	Routine as usual. 19 horses transferred sick to No.7 Veterinary Hospital. 4 horses admitted.	WJB

Army Form C. 2118.

WAR DIARY
or
INTELLIGENCE SUMMARY.
(Erase heading not required.)

Instructions regarding War Diaries and Intelligence Summaries are contained in F.S. Regs., Part II. and the Staff Manual respectively. Title pages will be prepared in manuscript.

Hour, Date, Place	Summary of Events and Information	Remarks and references to Appendices
BRESLE		
20 July 1916	Cpl Dexter returned to duty from Hospital. 2 horses admitted. WB	
21st " "	Float sent to No 1 M.V.S. & used by them to fetch horses, returned empty. 7 horses admitted WB	
22nd " "	5 horses admitted. WB	
23rd " "	8 Remounts drawn from FRECHENCOURT station for division. Arrangements made to evacuate tomorrow 7 horses admitted WB	
24th " "	25 cases transferred sick to No 7 Veterinary Hospital. Parade for inspection. 6 horses admitted WB	
25th " "	Routine as usual. Rifle drill. Float taken to I.O.M. Depot for repair of brake. WB	

Army Form C. 2118.

WAR DIARY
or
INTELLIGENCE SUMMARY.
(Erase heading not required.)

Instructions regarding War Diaries and Intelligence Summaries are contained in F.S. Regs., Part II. and the Staff Manual respectively. Title pages will be prepared in manuscript.

Hour, Date, Place	Summary of Events and Information	Remarks and references to Appendices
BRESLE		
26th July 1916	Routine as usual. 3 horses admitted. WJB	
" 27th "	Routine as usual. Rifle drill. 10 Remounts drawn from FRECHENCOURT. 3 horses admitted. WJB	
" 28th "	Routine as usual. Inspection of Kits etc. Remounts issued. 16 horses admitted. WJB	
" 29th "	Arrangements made to evacuate tomorrow. 15 horses admitted. WJB	
" 30th "	46 cases transferred sick to No 7 Veterinary Hospital. WJB	
" 31st "	Routine as usual. Arrangements made to move camp tomorrow. 4 horses admitted. WJB	

CONFIDENTIAL.

WAR DIARY
OF
44th MOBILE VETERINARY SECTION
34th DIVISION

From 1st August 1916 To 31st August 1916.

Volume 8.

Army Form C. 2118.

WAR DIARY
or
INTELLIGENCE SUMMARY.
(Erase heading not required.)

Instructions regarding War Diaries and Intelligence Summaries are contained in F.S. Regs., Part II. and the Staff Manual respectively. Title pages will be prepared in manuscript.

Hour, Date, Place	Summary of Events and Information	Remarks and references to Appendices
BRESLE 1st August 1916	Parade 9am & moved off from BRESLE to N20 entraining arrived 12.10pm Fraud camp. Cpl. Davis reported sick. 4 horses admitted	
Long Valley N20 2nd August 1916	127 Remounts arrived FRECHENCOURT 86 reach at station 41 brought to camp. Field Cashier Albert. 1000 francs from field cashier. 1 horse admitted	
Long Valley N20 3rd August 1916	Remounts issued & 8 more fetched from FRECHENCOURT. 11 horses admitted	
Long Valley N20 4th August 1916	21 Remounts collected from station. Remainder issued. 2 horses admitted	
Long Valley N20 5th August 1916	Arrangements made to evacuate tomorrow. Remounts issued. 6 horses admitted	
Long Valley N20 6th August 1916	25 cases transferred sick to No. 7 Veterinary Hospital from Mincourt. 4 horses admitted	

Army Form C. 2118.

WAR DIARY
or
INTELLIGENCE SUMMARY.
(Erase heading not required.)

Instructions regarding War Diaries and Intelligence Summaries are contained in F. S. Regs., Part II. and the Staff Manual respectively. Title pages will be prepared in manuscript.

Hour, Date, Place	Summary of Events and Information	Remarks and references to Appendices
Long Valley N20. 7th August 1916.	Routine as usual. Parade for inspection of kit, Rifles, etc. 3 Horses admitted. WyB.	
Long Valley. N20. 8th August 1916.	Routine as usual. 4 horses admitted. WyB.	
Long Valley N20. 9th August 1916.	Routine as usual. 19 horses admitted. WyB.	
Long Valley N20. 10th August 1916.	Routine as usual. Arrangements made to evacuate tomorrow. 4 horses admitted. WyB.	
Long Valley N20. 11th August 1916.	26 cases transferred sick to No. 1 Veterinary Hospital. 1 horse admitted. WyB.	
Long Valley N20. 12th August 1916.	Routine as usual. Parade for kit. 2 horses admitted. WyB.	
Long Valley N20. 13th August 1916.	Routine as usual. 13 horses admitted. WyB.	

Army Form C. 2118.

WAR DIARY
or
INTELLIGENCE SUMMARY.
(Erase heading not required.)

Instructions regarding War Diaries and Intelligence Summaries are contained in F. S. Regs., Part II. and the Staff Manual respectively. Title pages will be prepared in manuscript.

Hour, Date, Place	Summary of Events and Information	Remarks and references to Appendices
Long Valley. N.20. 14th August 1916.	Routine as usual. Recruits' class to move to BAIZIEUX on 16th inst. 2 horses admitted. WYB	
Long Valley. N.20. 15th August 1916.	Arrangements made to move tomorrow, 4 cases transferred to No. 5th Australian M.V.S., Two to No. 27th M.V.S., 4 to No. 2 M.V.S. WYB	
Long Valley N.20. 16th August 1916.	Parade of section 6.45. Moved off 9 am & marched to BAIZIEUX occupying billet no 7. Reported to A.D.V.S. WYB	
BAIZIEUX 17th August 1916.	Routine as usual. Orders received to await orders from C.O. R.A. as to move. WYB	
BAIZIEUX 18th August 1916.	Parade of section. Mounted 9 am for troop drill 2½ hrs. WYB	
BAIZIEUX 19th August 1916.	Routine as usual. Orders received to move with No 1, Coy A.S.C. to MORLANCOURT. WYB	

Army Form C. 2118.

WAR DIARY
or
INTELLIGENCE SUMMARY.
(Erase heading not required.)

Instructions regarding War Diaries and Intelligence Summaries are contained in F.S. Regs., Part II. and the Staff Manual respectively. Title pages will be prepared in manuscript.

Hour, Date, Place	Summary of Events and Information	Remarks and references to Appendices
BAIZIEUX 20th August 1916	Parade 9am, moved off 9.15 marched to QUERRIEU, bivouacking there for the night. WyB	
QUERRIEU 21st August 1916	Reveille 3.30 am. Parade 7 am moved off from camp marched to SALEAUX, bivouacing there for night. WyB	
SALEAUX 22nd August 1916.	Reveille 2.45 am. Parade 5 a.m. marched to station & entrained, section left 8.15 a.m. Arrived STEENBECQUE, 4-20 p.m. & detrained. marched from station 5.15 p.m. at DOULIEU bivouacing there, arrived 12.20 am. WyB	
23rd August 1916.	Reported to A.D.V.S. Parade 9am, marched to Biver on CROIX DU BAC. STEENWERCK road. at present attached by 30th M.V.S. 18th Division WyB	
CROIX-DU-BAC. 24th August 1916	Routine as usual. WyB	
CROIX-DU-BAC. 25th August 1916.	Took over from 30th M.V.S. also three horses two water troughs & maps. Parade for pay. 1 horse admitted WyB	

Army Form C. 2118.

WAR DIARY
or
INTELLIGENCE SUMMARY.
(Erase heading not required.)

Instructions regarding War Diaries and Intelligence Summaries are contained in F.S. Regs., Part II and the Staff Manual respectively. Title pages will be prepared in manuscript.

Hour, Date, Place	Summary of Events and Information	Remarks and references to Appendices
CROIX-DU-BAC. 26th August 1916.	Routine as usual. Scraping examined from horse of 22nd H. negative result. 6.30 pm horse of 62nd Bgde R.F.A. 18th Division. injected with mallein temperature 102.4. 5 horses admitted	WB
CROIX-DU-BAC. 27th August 1916	Routine as usual. A.D.V.S. inspected Section & billets. Scrapings taken from horse from No 1 Coy. A.S.C. No reaction to Mallein 4 horses admitted	WB WB
CROIX-DU-BAC. 28th August 1916.	Routine as usual. Horse returned to L Battery 152nd Bgde R.F.A. Cured. Arrangements made to evacuate by Barge tomorrow 9 horses admitted	WB
CROIX-DU-BAC. 29th August 1916.	6 horses transferred Sick to No 23. Veterinary Hospital St Omer. In all 32 horses loaded on barge Sgt. Proctor in charge. Arrangements made with 1.O.M. 5th Australians to alter float to take two horses abreast 1 horse admitted	WB
CROIX-DU-BAC. 30th August 1916.	Routine as usual. 10 places allotted on barge for tomorrows arrangements made to evacuate tomorrow back by road Barge Sgt Proctor reported back from St Omer 8.45 p.m. Telegram to say Barge late owing to bad weather. Horse of D.A.C. Mullioned 1 Horse admitted	WB

Army Form C. 2118.

WAR DIARY
or
INTELLIGENCE SUMMARY.
(Erase heading not required.)

Instructions regarding War Diaries and Intelligence Summaries are contained in F.S. Regs., Part II. and the Staff Manual respectively. Title pages will be prepared in manuscript.

Hour, Date, Place	Summary of Events and Information	Remarks and references to Appendices
Croix-Du-Bac. 31st August 1916.	Horse fetched in float from 15th Royal Scots. 16 cases transferred sick by barge to St Omer. Conducting party rationed horses foraged. Embarkation superintended. 5 cases transferred sick by road to No 6 V.H. Sgt Owen. 4 horses admitted. Sgts 10643 W Gimmell 27572 Spooner J. reported, attached.	W J Bainbridge / Capt. O.C. 4 M.V.S.

WAR DIARY
or
INTELLIGENCE SUMMARY.
(Erase heading not required.)

Army Form C. 2118.

Hour, Date, Place	Summary of Events and Information	Remarks and references to Appendices
CROIX-DU-BAC. 1st September.	Routine as usual. Parade for inspection of Rifles, Kit etc. Reinspected now killed. 1 Horse admitted.	
CROIX-DU-BAC. 2nd September.	Routine as usual. Estimates prepared for materials for building sheds at new site. 1 Horse admitted. No 75446 Sergt Sanders J.T. reported from to Sadery No.07 R.F.A. also 10993 Sgt Smith H. from C.B.Ducy 175 Bty R.A.	
CROIX-DU-BAC. 3rd September.	Routine as usual. Orders received to send H attached Sgt.5 to No 2. Veterinary Hospital Havre. Pte Duff No 11854. brought to Sadery Room & recd sick.	2 Horses admitted.
CROIX-DU-BAC. 4th September.	1000 Francs from Field Cashier. Routine as usual. H A.V.C. sergeants dispatched to No 2. Veterinary Hospt Havre. Paraded 5.45 am & sent to Steenwerck Station. Horse destroyed, No 3 Coy A.S.C. Sergt Owen returned from Dvt Duty.	5 Horses admitted

Army Form C. 2118.

WAR DIARY
or
INTELLIGENCE SUMMARY.
(Erase heading not required.)

Instructions regarding War Diaries and Intelligence Summaries are contained in F.S. Regs., Part II. and the Staff Manual respectively. Title pages will be prepared in manuscript.

Hour, Date, Place	Summary of Events and Information	Remarks and references to Appendices
Croix-Du-Bac. 5th September	Routine as usual, returned Anti-Gas School for instruction in use of respirators with an N.C.O. 2 Horses transferred sick by large Conducting Party having experimental conducting party rations. Horses foraged. 2 Horses admitted.	
Croix-Du-Bac. 6th September	Routine as usual, Arrangements made to transfer horses by large trained. 5 R.F.A. drivers to report for part of road party. Part of materials for buildings drawn from Erquinghem.	
Croix-Du-Bac. 7th September	5 cases transferred sick by large, loading foraging etc. superintended. 39 cases transferred sick by road to St. Omer. 19 animals transfd. ob. 102nd Field Ambulance. Materials for building drawn from E.M. 1 Horse admitted.	
Croix-Du-Bac. 8th September	Routine as usual. Parade for inspection of rifles, kit etc. also clothing. 2 Horses admitted.	

(73989) W.4141—463. 400,000. 9/14. H.&J.Ltd. Forms/C. 2118/10.

Army Form C. 2118.

WAR DIARY
or
INTELLIGENCE SUMMARY.
(Erase heading not required.)

Instructions regarding War Diaries and Intelligence Summaries are contained in F.S. Regs., Part II and the Staff Manual respectively. Title pages will be prepared in manuscript.

Hour, Date, Place	Summary of Events and Information	Remarks and references to Appendices
Croix-Du-Bac. 9th September.	Routine as usual. 21 miles 10th Lincolns. Braved. Parade for Pay. Pte Powett Niggins admitted to 104th Field Ambulance. Orders to move 75-magnount. 4 Horses admitted	
Croix-Du-Bac. 10th September	Parade 10.30 moved off from Billet to Field V.S.B.5th. Materials moved & building commenced. Pte Swan reported from Pt Drivers Driver Licence absent from night rollcall.	
Croix-Du-Bac. 11th September	Routine as usual. Building shed for forage, cook hut & men's huts. Escort sent to Stemment to Pt Licence P.S.C. Mgrh. Drl train acquainted Licence & application made for another arrest. Cpl Dent & party from Pt Drivers. Horses handed D-a.G. 21, 102 Field Ambc. 19, 21st North Tno. 26, P.S.C. 19. 6Horses admitted arrangements to transfer by Barge to-morrows.	
Croix-Du-Bac. 12th September.	5 cases transferred sick by barge. Road	

Army Form C. 2118.

WAR DIARY
or
INTELLIGENCE SUMMARY.
(Erase heading not required.)

Instructions regarding War Diaries and Intelligence Summaries are contained in F.S. Regs., Part II. and the Staff Manual respectively. Title pages will be prepared in manuscript.

Hour, Date, Place	Summary of Events and Information	Remarks and references to Appendices
CROIX-DU-BAC. 13th September	Pte Richardson kicked on barge Taken to No 2 Advanced C.C.S. at ESTAIRES. Reported to A.R.T.S. Dr Moreau reported to replace Licence Dr Licence returned to Bay. 13 Horses admitted.	W.M.B
CROIX-DU-BAC. 14th September	Animal destroyed at barge of 5th Australians. Branded horses of D.A.C. A.S.C. Bricks & felt roofing drawn from R.E. dump. 3 crates Transferred. Pick up barge. 1 Horse admitted.	W.M.B
CROIX-DU-BAC. 15th September	Horses of signals L.A.C. 123 north two. Branded. L.G.S. wagon sent for bricks none available. Finished building coke house. 1 Horse admitted.	W.M.B
CROIX-DU-BAC. 16th September	Routine as usual. Arrangements made to evacuate tomorrow. Box sent with Lieut Forbes's kit to 160 Bde R.F.A. 2 Horses admitted.	W.M.B
" 17th September	Routine as usual, G.S. wagon for timber 2 Horses admitted.	W.M.B

WAR DIARY
or
INTELLIGENCE SUMMARY.
(Erase heading not required.)

Army Form C. 2118.

Instructions regarding War Diaries and Intelligence Summaries are contained in F.S. Regts., Part II. and the Staff Manual respectively. Title pages will be prepared in manuscript.

Hour, Date, Place	Summary of Events and Information	Remarks and references to Appendices
Croix-du-Bac. 18th September	G.S. wagon sent for wire & timber. Dining room made for men. S.S. Younger discharged from hospital. Float sent to 103rd Field Ambulance. 2 Horses admitted.	
" 19th September	3 cases by barge. Pte Charlton admitted to Hospital. 1 Horse admitted.	
" 20th September	Ptes Power & Charlton discharged from Hospl. G.S. wagon sent for timber. 4 Horses admitted	
" 21st September	2 cases by road to St Omer. Two ammunition destroyed at Barge. so unfit to travel. Leaving & hovering unrepresented. 2 Horses returned to units. G.S. wagon for timber. 1 Horse admitted	
" 22nd September	13 Remounts collected from Bac St Maur Station. G.S. wagon for timber. 3 Horses admitted.	
" 23rd September	3 Remounts raised. G.S. wagon sent for timber. 2 Horses admitted.	

WAR DIARY or **INTELLIGENCE SUMMARY.**
(Erase heading not required.)

Army Form C. 2118.

Hour, Date, Place	Summary of Events and Information	Remarks and references to Appendices
CROIX-DU-BAC 24th September.	5 Remounts received. Routine as usual. 1 Horse admitted.	
" 25th September	4 Remounts received one taken in to Hospital lame. C.R.E. interviewed re stables. 1000 francs from Field Cashier. G.S. wagon top timber. Parade for pay. 7 Horses admitted.	
" 26th September	3 cases transferred sick ref Rough Loading etc. superintended. Timber drawn from Erquinghem. Pte Groom absent from 9.30 parade all day, reported awaiting to A.P.M. Ptes Wood & Bright reported from No.23 Veterinary Hospital. 4 Horses admitted	
" 27th September	Pte Groom returned to unit 8.45 a.m. E.S. wagon Finkel fetching stones all day. Pte Groom brought to Orderly room rewarded 28 days Field Punishment N.1. Sent to 104th Field Ambulance to be examined & then to A.P.M. for period. 3 Remounts drawn from /o. BREARDE 6 Horses admitted	

Army Form C. 2118.

WAR DIARY
or
INTELLIGENCE SUMMARY.
(Erase heading not required.)

Instructions regarding War Diaries and Intelligence Summaries are contained in F.S. Regs., Part II. and the Staff Manual respectively. Title pages will be prepared in manuscript.

Hour, Date, Place	Summary of Events and Information	Remarks and references to Appendices
Croix-DuBac 28th September	3 cases transferred Sick by Large Barge. Loading i/c. 275 cases beyond one remount sent. Stores drawn from camp of horses. 5 Horses admitted	WYB
" 29th September	Routine as usual. Float sent for horse at 51st Division. 2 Horses admitted	WYB
" 30th September	Routine as usual, one remount received 6 admitted	WYB

WYBainbridge/Capt. A.V.C.
O.C. 44 Mn V.S.

Vol 10

CONFIDENTIAL.

WAR DIARY.
OF
44th MOBILE VETERINARY SECTION.
34th DIVISION.

From. 1-10-16 To. 31-10-16

Volume. 10.

Army Form C. 2118.

WAR DIARY
or
INTELLIGENCE SUMMARY.
(Erase heading not required.)

Instructions regarding War Diaries and Intelligence Summaries are contained in F.S. Regs., Part II. and the Staff Manual respectively. Title pages will be prepared in manuscript.

Hour, Date, Place	Summary of Events and Information	Remarks and references to Appendices
CROIX-DU-BAC. 1st October 1916	Routine as usual. 2 horses destroyed. G.S. wagon sent for bricks. Travelling horse sent to LA BREARDE. Sie Kills proceed on 10 days. Special leave. Started building stables. 2 horses admitted. MyB.	
" 2nd October 1916	Cpl Clint despatched to No. 12. Veterinary Hospital, for instruction clipping etc. G.S. wagon sent for bricks. MyB. Mule Tetanus destroyed. 1 horse admitted.	
" 3rd October 1916	13 cases Transferred Sick by barge. Conducting party found horses forage loading superintended. MyB. G.S. wagon sent for bricks. Building continued. 15 Horses admitted.	
" 4th October 1916	Routine as usual. G.S. wagon sent for bricks. Cpl Clint returned from No. 12. Veterinary Hospital. Building stables. 1 horse admitted. MyB.	
" 5th October 1916	13 cases Transferred Sick by barge. Conducting party found forage loading superintended. Bricks from ERQUINGHEM G.S. wagon. Building stables. 6 Horses admitted. MyB.	

Army Form C. 2118.

WAR DIARY
or
INTELLIGENCE SUMMARY.
(Erase heading not required.)

Instructions regarding War Diaries and Intelligence Summaries are contained in F.S. Regs., Part II. and the Staff Manual respectively. Title pages will be prepared in manuscript.

Hour, Date, Place	Summary of Events and Information	Remarks and references to Appendices
CROIX-DU-BAC. 6th October 1916	Routine as usual. G.S. wagon sent to ARMENTIERES for wood, also barrel of tar for Bricks at night. Building of stables continued. WWB	
" 7th October 1916	Routine as usual. Building stables. G.S. wagon for bricks. Paraded all ranks. 2 Horses admitted. WWB	
" 8th October 1916	Horse fetched in float from No.3 Coy. A.S.C. Building continued. 5 Horses admitted. WWB	
" 9th October 1916	Routine as usual. G.S. wagon sent for bricks. 5 Horses admitted. Building continued. WWB	
" 10th October 1916	10 cases Transferred Sick by barge. wagon superintended loading. Horses foraged. G.S. for bricks. Building continued. WWB	
" 11th October 1916	Routine as usual. Ptes Wood & Bright inoculated. G.S. wagon for bricks. 7 Horses admitted. WWB	

WAR DIARY
or
INTELLIGENCE SUMMARY.
(Erase heading not required.)

Army Form C. 2118.

Instructions regarding War Diaries and Intelligence Summaries are contained in F.S. Regs., Part II. and the Staff Manual respectively. Title pages will be prepared in manuscript.

Hour, Date, Place	Summary of Events and Information	Remarks and references to Appendices
CROIX-DU-BAC		
12th October 1916	Routine as usual. Box Respirators issued to all ranks. 1 file. Wells reported off leave. G.S. wagon for bricks. Building continued. WWB	
13th October 1916	9 cases Transferred Sick, by barge. Parade for inspection of rifles etc, practice in new Anti-Gas Respirators 45 minutes. Building continued. WWB	
14th October 1916	Routine as usual. G.S. wagon for bricks. Building continued. 1 Horse admitted. WWB	
15th October 1916	Routine as usual. G.S. wagon for bricks. Building continued. 2 Horses admitted. WWB	
16th October 1916	Routine as usual. G.S. wagon for bricks. Building continued. 3 Horses admitted. WWB	

Army Form C. 2118.

WAR DIARY
or
INTELLIGENCE SUMMARY.
(Erase heading not required.)

Instructions regarding War Diaries and Intelligence Summaries are contained in F.S. Regs., Part II. and the Staff Manual respectively. Title pages will be prepared in manuscript.

Hour, Date, Place	Summary of Events and Information	Remarks and references to Appendices
CROIX-DU-BAC.		
17th October 1916	Routine as usual. Felt drawn from R.E. yard Roofing of stables continued. 9 cases Transferred Sick by barge, loading etc superintended. Horse D.A.C. destroyed. 2 Horses admitted WJB	
" 18th October 1916	Routine as usual. C.R.E. inspected stables 9 floats G.S. wagon for bricks. Building continued. WJB 8 Horses admitted.	
" 19th October 1916	12 cases Transferred Sick, 6 by barge, 6 by road. Cpl Offord put under arrest & sent to A.P.M. to guard room for night. G.S. wagon for bricks. WJB	
" 20th October 1916	Routine as usual. Parade for inspection & drill with Box Respirators. Cpl Cent brought to Orderly Room & dealt with. Pte Bishop admitted to 10th Fld Ambulance. 3 Horses admitted. WJB	
" 21st October 1916	Routine as usual. Building continued WJB	

Army Form C. 2118.

WAR DIARY
or
INTELLIGENCE SUMMARY.
(Erase heading not required.)

Instructions regarding War Diaries and Intelligence Summaries are contained in F.S. Regs., Part II. and the Staff Manual respectively. Title pages will be prepared in manuscript.

Hour, Date, Place	Summary of Events and Information	Remarks and references to Appendices
CROIX-DU-BAC.		
22nd October 1916	Routine as usual. Pte Bishop reported for duty from 104th Field Ambley. Sgt Owen went on Special Leave. 2 Horses admitted.	W.B.
23rd October 1916	Routine as usual. 44 Remounts collected from BAILLEUL Station, issued to units. Building continued. 10 Horses admitted.	W.B.
24th October 1916	Routine as usual. Pte Groom sent for from A.S.M. Completion of punishment. No. S.E. 416 97 S.S. Sigley reported from No. 20 M.V.S. for duty. 14 Cases Transferred Sick by barge. 2 Horses admitted.	W.B.
25th October 1916	Routine as usual. Pte Broom despatched to No. 23 Veterinary Hospital. 1 Horse admitted.	W.B.
26th October 1916	Routine as usual. Float sent to I.O.M. 2nd ANZACS. Cpl. S.S. Younger despatched to No. 4 Veterinary Hospital on promotion. Building continued.	W.B.

Army Form C. 2118.

WAR DIARY
or
INTELLIGENCE SUMMARY.
(Erase heading not required.)

Instructions regarding War Diaries and Intelligence Summaries are contained in F.S. Regs., Part II. and the Staff Manual respectively. Title pages will be prepared in manuscript.

Hour, Date, Place	Summary of Events and Information	Remarks and references to Appendices
CROIX-DU-BAC. 27th October 1916	Routine as usual. G.S. wagon for fascines also Bricks. 2 Horses Transferred Sick by barge. WB. Loading Foraging superintended.	
" 28th October 1916	Routine as usual. Section horses put into Stables. G.S. wagon for coke stores. WB. 5 Horses admitted.	
" 29th October 1916	Routine as usual. Parade for inspection & Gas Helmet drill. Clothing etc indents submitted Pte Turnbull admitted to 104th Fld Amble. WB. 3 Horses admitted.	
" 30th October 1916	Routine as usual. Indents for pumps & troughs re Instructions from C.R.E. WB. G.S. wagon for bricks.	
" 31st October 1916	A.A. & Q.M.G. inspected section billets 6 Cases Transferred sick by barge G.S. wagon for bricks. 2 Horses admitted.	

W.B. Bainbridge / Capt. A.V.C.
O.C. 14th Mobile Veterinary Section

CONFIDENTIAL.

WAR DIARY.

OF

44th MOBILE VETERINARY SECTION

34th DIVISION.

From 1-11-16. To 30-11-16.

Volume. II.

Army Form C. 2118.

WAR DIARY
or
INTELLIGENCE SUMMARY.
(Erase heading not required.)

Instructions regarding War Diaries and Intelligence Summaries are contained in F.S. Regs., Part II and the Staff Manual respectively. Title pages will be prepared in manuscript.

Hour, Date, Place	Summary of Events and Information	Remarks and references to Appendices
Croix Du Bac. 1st November 1916	Routine as usual. 3 Horses admitted. WWB	
2nd " "	Routine as usual. Building stables making roads. 5 Horses admitted. WWB	
3rd " "	Routine as usual. 8 cases transferred sick by Barge. Loading superintended. Forage provided. Float sent for from I.O.M. repairs. 5 horses reported off lame. Parade for pay. WWB	
4th " "	Routine as usual. Demonstration by A.D.V.S. to all F.O. Wagon line, Officers & N.C.Os of the Division. Pte Dutchtel reported from 10th F.A. Amb. CC. WWB 1 Horse admitted	
5th " "	Routine as usual. Parade for inspection of rifles etc. Respractice with Gas Helmets. 2 Horses returned. Punt from R.E.S. float for horse of 152nd R.F.A. 7 Horses admitted. WWB	

Army Form C. 2118.

WAR DIARY
or
INTELLIGENCE SUMMARY.
(Erase heading not required.)

Hour, Date, Place	Summary of Events and Information	Remarks and references to Appendices
CROIX-DU-BAC. 6th November 1916.	Routine as usual. Building huts etc. G.S. wagon for trucks. 14 Horses admitted. WJB	
" 7th " "	Routine as usual. 8 Horses transferred Lieut by Barge. Loading superintended. Horses forayed. WJB	
" 8th " "	Routine as usual. Bricks drawn G.S. wagon. Simple feared from STEENWERCK. 10 Horses received from 7th Divl M.T.S. 10 Horses admitted. WJB	
" 9th " "	Routine as usual. Pte Ellis admitted 15-10-16. Field Ambce. Flooring of stabling finished. 2 Horses admitted. WJB	
" 10th " "	9 Horses transferred Sect by road to St OMER. Started building dressing for forage. G.S.wagon for Bricks. Barge did not sail. 3 Horses from 25th Divn. 3 Horses admitted. WJB	

Army Form C. 2118.

WAR DIARY
or
INTELLIGENCE SUMMARY.
(Erase heading not required.)

Instructions regarding War Diaries and Intelligence Summaries are contained in F.S. Regs., Part II and the Staff Manual respectively. Title pages will be prepared in manuscript.

Hour, Date, Place	Summary of Events and Information	Remarks and references to Appendices
Croix du Bac. 11th November 1916.	Routine as usual. Bureau continued. Linseed cake fetched & timber from Bailleul. WAB	
12" " "	Routine as usual. Chaff cutter repaired. Forage fetched. 9 horses admitted. WAB	
13" " "	Routine as usual. Pte Ellis reported from 10th Bde Ambce returned to duty. 5 horses admitted. WAB	
14" " "	Routine as usual. 24 horses transferred. Sick by Barge. Loading superintended. Sgt Owen admitted to 10th Fd Ambce. 2 horses admitted. WAB	
15" " "	Routine as usual. Parade for inspection of rifles, helmets etc. 3 horse admitted. WAB	
16" " "	Routine as usual. 6 horses admitted. WAB	

Army Form C. 2118.

WAR DIARY
or
INTELLIGENCE SUMMARY.
(Erase heading not required.)

Instructions regarding War Diaries and Intelligence Summaries are contained in F.S. Regs., Part II. and the Staff Manual respectively. Title pages will be prepared in manuscript.

Hour, Date, Place	Summary of Events and Information	Remarks and references to Appendices
CROIX-DU-BAC.		
17th November 1916	Routine as usual. Parade for pay. 5 horses Transferred. Sick by Road. 1 to H.y Barge. 2 horses admitted. WMB	
18" "	Routine as usual. All vehicles moved with Divl. Sign wire previous place. 2 horses admitted. WMB	
19" "	Routine as usual. Arrangements made with O.C. 104th Fld Amblce. to inoculate all ranks of Section. 3 Remounts drawn from H.A. BREARDE. 4 horses admitted. WMB	
20" "	Routine as usual. 3 men inoculated at 104th Fld Amblce. 1 mess case from BAILLEUL. 2 horses admitted. WMB	
21st "	Routine as usual. Remount parade. 2 horses Waived to duty. 7 cases Transferred Sick by Barge. Loading Morning supervised. WMB	

Army Form C. 2118.

WAR DIARY
or
INTELLIGENCE SUMMARY.
(Erase heading not required.)

Instructions regarding War Diaries and Intelligence Summaries are contained in F.S. Regs., Part II. and the Staff Manual respectively. Title pages will be prepared in manuscript.

Hour, Date, Place	Summary of Events and Information	Remarks and references to Appendices
CROIX-DU-BAC. 22nd November 1916	Routine as usual. 3 men evacuated. Pte Turnbull remitted to 104th Fd Amb'ce. 6 horses admitted. MWB	
23rd November 1916	Routine as usual. 3 men evacuated. 2 horses admitted. MWB	
24th " "	7 cases transferred sick by barge, loading superintended. Sgt Owen reported from 104th Fd Amb'ce. Pte Power admitted to 104th Fd Amb'ce. MWB	
25th " "	20 Remounts drawn from B.A.C. ST MAUR Station. 5 evacd. 1 horse admitted. MWB	
26th " "	Routine as usual. Sgt Proctor granted 10 days leave. 7 horses admitted. MWB	
27th " "	Routine as usual. Pte Paul admitted to Hospital. 13 horses admitted. MWB	

WAR DIARY
or
INTELLIGENCE SUMMARY.

(Erase heading not required.)

Army Form C. 2118.

Hour, Date, Place	Summary of Events and Information	Remarks and references to Appendices
CROIX-DU-BAC. 28th November 1916	Routine as usual. 15 cases transferred Sect by Barge, loading etc superintended. WB. 5 Horses admitted.	
29th "	Routine as usual. Shoeing lanterns drawn from Salvage dump. Horse died (3nm Aust D.v.) Pte's Power & Turnbull reported from 104th Fld Amb. WB. 14 Horses admitted.	
30th "	Routine as usual. D.D.V.S. 2nd Armies inspected Section. Demonstration on fitting of plates to prevent horses upsetting. 2 Horses admitted.	

J.W. Saunders / Capt. A.V.C.
O.C. 44 M.V.S.

Vol 12

CONFIDENTIAL

WAR DIARY

44th MOBILE VETERINARY SECTION.

34th DIVISION.

From 1st December 1916 to 31st December 1916

(Volume 12.)

WAR DIARY
or
INTELLIGENCE SUMMARY.
(Erase heading not required.)

Army Form C. 2118.

Instructions regarding War Diaries and Intelligence Summaries are contained in F.S. Regs., Part II. and the Staff Manual respectively. Title pages will be prepared in manuscript.

Hour, Date, Place 1916	Summary of Events and Information	Remarks and references to Appendices
Croix du Bac Dec. 1st	Routine as usual. 4 Horses Transferred Sick by Boat & 12 Holes by Barge. Foraging & Loading of Barge Superintended. WB	
" " " 2nd	Routine as usual. Mule returned to 15th. Royal Scots. WB	
" " " 3rd	Routine as usual. 1 Case admitted. WB	
" " " 4th	Routine as usual. 1500 Francs Field Cashier. Fascines drawn from Royal Engineers Yard, Sawdust drawn from Royal Engineers Yard at Sailly Notta. 5 Cases admitted WB	
Croix du Bac " 5th	Routine as usual 12 Cases Transferred Sick by Barge. Foraging & Loading of Barge Superintended. 4 Cases admitted. WB	
" " " 6th	Routine as usual. Load of Tins fetched from L'Epinette. 2 Cases admitted. WB	

WAR DIARY
or
INTELLIGENCE SUMMARY.
(Erase heading not required.)

Army Form C. 2118.

Hour, Date, Place 1916	Summary of Events and Information	Remarks and references to Appendices
" Dec. 1st	Routine as usual. Parade for inspection of Rifles &c. Gas helmets exercises. This from 2 Epinette & S Waggon for Bricks WJB	
Croix Du Bac " 8th	Routine as usual. 10 Cases Transferred Sick by Barge. Foraging & Loading of Barge Superintended. 2 Cases admitted. WJB	
" " 9th	Routine as usual. Sgt. Proctor reported from leave WJB	
" " 10th	Routine as usual. 3 Remounts drawn from Bac St Maur Station. S.S. Sigley granted leave. 1 admitted. WJB	
" " 11th	Routine as usual. 9 Remounts collected from La Bricarde. 1000 Francs Field Cashier WJB	
" " 12th	Routine as usual. 1 Remount issued. 2 Cases Transferred Sick by Barge. Foraging & Loading of Barge Superintended. 2 Cases admitted WJB	

WAR DIARY
or
INTELLIGENCE SUMMARY.
(Erase heading not required.)

Army Form C. 2118.

Instructions regarding War Diaries and Intelligence Summaries are contained in F.S. Regs., Part II and the Staff Manual respectively. Title pages will be prepared in manuscript.

Hour, Date, Place	Summary of Events and Information	Remarks and references to Appendices
Dec. 13th 1916	Routine as usual. 2 Remounts issued to Capt Manley. Mule sent to Field Remount Section La Brigade. 5 Cases admitted. WJB	
" 14th	Routine as usual. G.S. waggon for Bricks & Cases admitted. WJB	
Croix Du Bac 15th	Routine as usual. 9 Cases. Transferred sick to Barge. Foraging & Loading of Barge Superintended. WJB	
" 16th	Routine as usual. Parade for pay etc. WJB	
" 17th	Routine as Usual. Cpl. Gent. proceeded to England on leave. Timber drawn from Royal Engineers Yard. 2 Cases admitted. WJB	
" 18th	Routine as usual. 1000 Francs. Field Cashier. 4 Cases admitted. WJB	

Army Form C. 2118.

WAR DIARY
or
INTELLIGENCE SUMMARY.
(Erase heading not required.)

Hour, Date, Place 1916	Summary of Events and Information	Remarks and references to Appendices
Croix du Bac December 19th	Routine as usual. 5 Cases transferred Sick by Barge. Foraging & Loading of Barge Superintended	WB
" " 20th	Routine as usual. Pte. J. Duff admitted to 104th Field Ambulance. 3 Cases admitted.	WB
" " 21st	Routine as usual. 99 Sgt. J.E. Harper. 9.3387. Pte. Sturch reported for duty from No 9 Veterinary Hospital. 8 cases Evacuated by road 8 cases Transferred Sick by Barge. Foraging & Loading Superintended.	WB
" " 22nd	Routine as usual. 1 case admitted	WB
Croix du Bac. 23rd	Routine as usual. 4 Cases Transferred Sick by Barge. Foraging & Loading Superintended 1 Case admitted	WB

WAR DIARY
or
INTELLIGENCE SUMMARY.
(Erase heading not required.)

Army Form C. 2118.

Hour, Date, Place	Summary of Events and Information	Remarks and references to Appendices
Dec. 24th 1916	Routine as usual 1 case admitted WyB	
" 25th	Routine as usual.	
" 26th	Routine as usual. WyB	
" 27th	Routine as usual. 2 cases admitted. WyB	
" 28th	Routine as usual. No 29. Sgt Owen & No 8 & 2 Cpl Hunting despatched to No 9. Veterinary Hospital 1 case admitted WyB	
Croix du Bac " 29th	Routine as usual 9 G.S. waggon for Bricks 1 case admitted. WyB	
" 30th	Routine as usual. 6 cases transferred Sick by Barge. Foraging & Loading Superintended 2 cases admitted. WyB	
" 31st	Routine as usual. 1 case admitted. WyB	
	Routine as usual 5. cases admitted	

W Bowlending / Capt a. Vc
b C 44 M.C.S.

Vol 13

Confidental War Diary

of

44ᵀᴴ Mobile Vet: Section.

34ᵀᴴ Division

From Jan: 1ˢᵗ 1917. To Jan. 31ˢᵗ 1917

Volume 13.

WAR DIARY
or
INTELLIGENCE SUMMARY.
(Erase heading not required.)

Army Form C. 2118.

Instructions regarding War Diaries and Intelligence Summaries are contained in F.S. Regs., Part II and the Staff Manual respectively. Title pages will be prepared in manuscript.

Hour, Date, Place	Summary of Events and Information	Remarks and references to Appendices
1.1.19. Croix Du Bac.	Routine as usual. 3 men sent to 104th Field Ambulance for Inoculation. 5 cases admitted. WMB	
2.1.19 " "	Routine as usual. 3 men sent to 104th Field Ambulance for Inoculation. Horse discharged. Rue 5 francs. Barge "Eboness" sailing owing to floods. 1 case admitted. WMB	
3.1.19 " "	Routine as usual. 13 men sent to baths at Erquing-hem. also their blankets for disinfection. 5 cases admitted. WMB	
4.1.19 " "	Routine as usual. Pte Power reported from leave. Inspection of Clothing. 4 cases admitted. WMB	
5.1.19 " "	Routine as usual. 12 Mange cases evacuated by road - 4 by barge. Foraging and loading barge. Mule destroyed. 3 cases admitted. WMB	
6.1.19 " "	Routine as usual. 8 cases admitted. WMB	
7.1.19 " "	Routine as usual. Parade for inspection of Rifles. Gas Helmet Drill. Pte Smith admitted to Hospital. 6 cases admitted. WMB	
8.1.19 " "	Routine as usual. 9 cases admitted. WMB	

Army Form C. 2118.

WAR DIARY
or
INTELLIGENCE SUMMARY.
(Erase heading not required.)

Instructions regarding War Diaries and Intelligence Summaries are contained in F.S. Regs., Part II. and the Staff Manual respectively. Title pages will be prepared in manuscript.

Hour, Date, Place	Summary of Events and Information	Remarks and references to Appendices
9-1-14 Croix Du Bac	Routine as usual. 6 cases transferred sick by barge. Loading & foraging barge. 2 cases admitted.	
10-1-14 "	Routine as usual. Horse destroyed. Tetanus. 6 cases admitted.	
11-1-14 "	Routine as usual. Parade for inspection of Rifles Etc. & Gas Helmet Drill. Horse destroyed. fractured tibia. 8 cases admitted.	
12-1-14 "	Routine as usual. 14 Horses transferred sick by road & 14 by barge. Loading, foraging, etc of barge.	
13-1-14 "	Routine as usual. 3 Horses returned to Units. 10 Remounts drawn from Bac-St-Maur station & issued to Units. 5 cases admitted.	
14-1-14 "	Routine as usual. 1 case admitted.	
15-1-14 "	Routine as usual. 1,000 Francs from Field Cashier. Float sent to 103rd Brigade Head Qrs. for horse. 1 Horse returned to Unit. Surplus Mule sent to Remount Section. No Parade. 11. cases admitted.	
16-1-14 "	Routine as usual. Horse destroyed 103rd B/64? Gnr. He. Smith reported for duty from our Field Ambulance. Lumbago sent to Bailleul for care. 8 cases admitted.	

WAR DIARY
or
INTELLIGENCE SUMMARY.
(Erase heading not required.)

Army Form C. 2118.

Instructions regarding War Diaries and Intelligence Summaries are contained in F.S. Regs., Part II and the Staff Manual respectively. Title pages will be prepared in manuscript.

Hour, Date, Place	Summary of Events and Information	Remarks and references to Appendices
14..1..14. Cavce. Div. Bac.	Routine as usual. Chestnut Horse returned from Cap. Tellett. 3 cases admitted WWB.	
18..1..14 " "	Routine as usual. 5 cases admitted WWB.	
19..1..14 " "	Routine as usual. 12 cases transferred sick by road & 13 by barge. Two barges loaded. (63 Horses) foraging etc. 8 cases admitted WWB.	
20..1..14 " "	Routine as usual. Boat sent to St Jans Capel for quicklime WWB.	
21..1..14 " "	Routine as usual. Pte Charlton granted leave to Chantilly. 1 case admitted WWB.	
22..1..14 " "	Routine as usual. 4 cases admitted WWB.	
23..1..14 " "	Routine as usual. Orders from D.D.V.S. that M.V.S. would supply Quicksum with Calcium Sulphide. 6 casks evacuated by barge foraging foraging barge. 1 case admitted WWB.	
24..1..14 " "	Routine as usual. Arrangements made to draw Soya Stove from R.E. and coal for same from S.S.6. 2 cases admitted WWB.	
25..1..14 " "	Routine as usual. Stove and coal drawn & Calcium Sulphide made. Parade all ranks for pay. 4 cases admitted WWB.	
26..1..14 " "	Routine as usual. 2 Mange cases evacuated by road & 4 cases by barge. foraging loading etc of barge. No hay available. Oats only 24 Horbag supplied to 6 barge loading orders at H. 30. P.V. to 6 ready to move at one hours notice later 6 P.M. Orders to await instructions from 6.06. P.A. Arrangements made with 8th Cav. M.V.S. to take cases in Hospital. 1 case admitted WWB.	

Army Form C. 2118.

WAR DIARY
or
INTELLIGENCE SUMMARY.
(Erase heading not required.)

Instructions regarding War Diaries and Intelligence Summaries are contained in F.S. Regs., Part II and the Staff Manual respectively. Title pages will be prepared in manuscript.

Hour, Date, Place	Summary of Events and Information	Remarks and references to Appendices
24.1.14 Croix Du Bac	Routine as usual. 5 Cases sent to 3rd Cycl. M.T.S. Orders to stand fast until further notice. Waggons Etc packed. 1923. visited Section 5 Pln. 4 Cases admitted. WyB	
28.1.14 Croix Du Bac	Routine as usual. WyB	
29.1.14 Croix Du Bac	Routine as usual. Corp. Dexter reported from S. Omer. WyB	
30.1.14 Croix Du Bac	Routine as usual. Inspection of Gas Helmets. WyB	
31.1.14 Croix Du Bac	Routine as usual. WyB	

W. Bainbridge / Capt.
O.C. 14th M.T.S.

Confidetial

War Diary
of
44ᵗʰ Mobile
Veterinary Section
34ᵗʰ Division

From Feb: 1ˢᵗ 1917
To Feb: 28ᵗʰ 1917.

Army Form C. 2118.

WAR DIARY
or
INTELLIGENCE SUMMARY.
(Erase heading not required.)

Instructions regarding War Diaries and Intelligence Summaries are contained in F.S.Regs., Part II and the Staff Manual respectively. Title pages will be prepared in manuscript.

Hour, Date, Place	Summary of Events and Information	Remarks and references to Appendices
CROIX-DU-BAC. 1.2.19.	Routine as usual. Parade for Inspection & Rifle Drill. WB	
" 2.2.19	Routine as usual. Parade all Ranks and Rifle Drill. WB	
" 3.2.19	Routine as usual. Parade for Gas helmets and Rifle Drill. WB	
" 4.2.19	Routine as usual. Orderly sent to 115th for Warrants for leave men. WB	
" 5.2.19	Routine as usual. 1,000 francs drawn from Field Cashier Bailleul, Leave for two men cancelled. Rifle Drill. WB	
" 6.2.19	Routine as usual. Ptes Huggins & Massey granted leave. WB	
" 7.2.19	Routine as usual. Parade for Rifle Drill. WB	
" 8.2.19	Routine as usual. WB	
" 9.2.19	Routine as usual. WB	

Army Form C. 2118.

WAR DIARY
or
INTELLIGENCE SUMMARY.
(Erase heading not required.)

Instructions regarding War Diaries and Intelligence Summaries are contained in F.S. Regs., Part II. and the Staff Manual respectively. Title pages will be prepared in manuscript.

Hour, Date, Place	Summary of Events and Information	Remarks and references to Appendices
CROIX DU BAC. 10.2.14.	Routine as usual, Parade for Pay. 1 Case Admitted	WB
11.2.14	Routine as usual. 4 Cases Admitted	WB
12.2.14	Routine as usual. 1 float sent to "B" Bt att 152 Bde R.F.A. 1,000 francs drawn from Field Cashier. 14 Cases Admitted	WB
13.2.14	Routine as usual. 9 Cases. Trams sent by Road. 1 foal	WB
14.2.14	Routine as usual.	WB
15.2.14	Routine as usual	WB
16.2.14	Routine as usual	WB
17.2.14	Routine as usual. Orders received to move from billets on 19th. Arrangements made with A.D.V.S. 3rd Aus. & M.V.S. to take over cases. 6 Cases Admitted	WB

WAR DIARY
or
INTELLIGENCE SUMMARY.

(Erase heading not required.)

Army Form C. 2118.

Instructions regarding War Diaries and Intelligence Summaries are contained in F.S. Regs., Part II. and the Staff Manual respectively. Title pages will be prepared in manuscript.

Hour, Date, Place		Summary of Events and Information	Remarks and references to Appendices
CROIX-DU-BAC	18.2.14	Arrangements made to move to-morrow, 15 Cases handed over to 3rd Aust M.V.S. 2 Cases Admitted. WB.	
"	19.2.14	Reveille 6.A.M. Parade 4.45.A.M. Marched off from billet to starting point, and passed at 9.A.M. Arrived at STEENBECQUE 4.20 P.M. Billeted. Corp. Gent dispatched to Fontes as billeting party. WB	
STEENBECQUE	20.2.14	Reveille 6.30 A.M. Parade 11.45. Marched off 12 noon & passed starting point 12.50. Arrived FONTES 3.15 P.M. Billeted. WB	
FONTES	21.2.14	Reveille 6 A.M. Corp. S. Gent & Breeton sent to NOYELLES as billeting party. Parade 9.15 A.M. Marched off 9.30 & passed starting point at 9.45. arrived NOYELLES 3.15 P.M. & billeted. WB	
NOYELLES	22.2.14	Reveille 6.30 a.m. Parade for Inspection of Rifles & Saddlery at c.t.f.c. WB	
	23.2.14	Routine as usual WB	
	24.2.14	Routine as usual WB	

Army Form C. 2118.

WAR DIARY
or
INTELLIGENCE SUMMARY.
(Erase heading not required.)

Instructions regarding War Diaries and Intelligence Summaries are contained in F.S. Regs., Part II. and the Staff Manual respectively. Title pages will be prepared in manuscript.

Hour, Date, Place	Summary of Events and Information	Remarks and references to Appendices
NOYELLES 25.2.17	Routine as usual	
26.2.17	Routine as usual	
27.2.17	Routine as usual, Ptes. Huggins & Macey reported from leave	
28.2.17	Routine as usual. Cpl. Gent & 3 men sent to "A" Batt. 152 Bde R.F.A. to collect 4 sick Horses & take same to 21st A.V.S. at AUBIGNY.	

W.J. Bainbridge Capt. A.V.C.
O.C. 44 M.V.S.

Vol 15

CONFIDENTIAL.

WAR DIARY

OF.

44TH M.V.S.

34TH DIVISION.

FROM.

MARCH 1ST 1917. TO. MARCH. 31ST 1917.

Army Form C. 2118.

WAR DIARY
or
INTELLIGENCE SUMMARY.
(Erase heading not required.)

Instructions regarding War Diaries and Intelligence Summaries are contained in F.S. Regs., Part II. and the Staff Manual respectively. Title pages will be prepared in manuscript.

Place	Hour, Date	Summary of Events and Information	Remarks and references to Appendices
NOYELLES.	1. 3. 19.	Routine as usual. Parade 2.P.M. for inspection of Rifles Etc, Gas excuses with Box Respirators. MWB.	
"	2. 3. 19	Received Orders at 8.45A.M. to march to Villers Brulin, leave at 10.45 A.M. Corpl Gent sent to Villers Brulin as billeting party. Parade 10.30AM. Marched off from billet. Met en route by dispatch rider with orders to proceed to LA. THIEULOYE. Reported to Theuloye & billeted there. Reported personally to 101st Inf. Bde. H.Q. MWB.	
LA. THIEULOYE.	3. 3. 19	Routine as usual. Inspection of Rifles Etc. MWB.	
"	4. 3. 19	Routine as usual. MWB.	
"	5. 3. 19	Routine as usual. Parade for foot drill. MWB.	
"	6. 3. 19	Routine as usual. 4 Surplus Horses sent to M.T.S. for inspection as to fitness for re-issue to Division. MWB.	
"	7. 3. 19	Routine as usual. MWB.	
"	8. 3. 19	Routine as usual. MWB.	

Army Form C. 2118.

WAR DIARY
or
INTELLIGENCE SUMMARY.
(Erase heading not required.)

Instructions regarding War Diaries and Intelligence Summaries are contained in F.S. Regs., Part II. and the Staff Manual respectively. Title pages will be prepared in manuscript.

Hour, Date, Place	Summary of Events and Information	Remarks and references to Appendices
LA THIEULOYE. 9.3.19.	Routine as usual. Parade for pay. WB	
" 10.3.19.	Routine as usual. Parade for drill. WB	
" 11.3.19.	Routine as usual. Steel Helmets drawn from Ordnance & issued. WB	
" 12.3.19.	Routine as usual. Orders received to move to VILLERS BRULIN tomorrow. WB	
" 13.3.19.	Reveille 6.30 a.m. Parade 9.15 a.m. and moved off from billets. Arrived at VILLERS BRULIN. 1.15 P.M. and billeted. WB	
VILLERS BRULIN 14.3.19	Moved from billet to one more suitable in Villers Brulin. 1 case admitted. WB	
" 15.3.19	Routine as usual. Parade for inspection. WB	
" 16.3.19	Routine as usual. Route marched out & reconnoitred from proposed A.C.P. to AGNIERES. 1 case admitted. WB	
" 19.3.19	Routine as usual. P/G. AUBIGNY interviewed, reference using that station as Railhead, also G.S.O. 1 case admitted. WB	

Army Form C. 2118.

WAR DIARY
or
INTELLIGENCE SUMMARY.
(Erase heading not required.)

Instructions regarding War Diaries and Intelligence Summaries are contained in F.S. Regs., Part II. and the Staff Manual respectively. Title pages will be prepared in manuscript.

Hour, Date, Place	Summary of Events and Information	Remarks and references to Appendices
VILLERS BRULIN 18. 3. 14	Routine as usual. Shed at billet collapses. Reported same to D.V.H.P 6.S. 10 Cases admitted. W.J.B.	
19. 3. 14.	Routine as usual. Two Horses destroyed 25 Cases admitted W.J.B.	
20. 3. 14.	Routine as usual. Arrangements made to evacuate sick horses tomorrow. One mule destroyed W.J.B.	
21. 3. 14	30. Cases transferred sick from AUBIGNY station to 22nd Vet Hosp. W.J.B.	
22. 3. 14	Routine as usual. S.S. Sigley admitted to 103rd Field Ambulance. W.J.B.	
23. 3. 14	Routine as usual. Lt. Gent reported from ABBEVILLE with conducting party. Parade for pay. Journalling admitted from A.P.M. W.J.B.	
24. 3. 14	Routine as usual. Parade for inspection of Gas helmet anti W.J.B.	
25. 3. 14	Routine as usual. Horse sent to No. 3. Sec. D.A.C. for Mule. W.J.B.	
26. 3. 14.	Routine as usual. 51 Cases admitted including 43 from D.A.C. W.J.B.	

(73989) W4141—463. 400,000. 9/14. H.&J.Ltd. Forms/C. 2118/10.

Army Form C. 2118.

WAR DIARY
or
INTELLIGENCE SUMMARY.
(Erase heading not required.)

Instructions regarding War Diaries and Intelligence Summaries are contained in F.S. Regs., Part II and the Staff Manual respectively. Title pages will be prepared in manuscript.

Place	Hour, Date	Summary of Events and Information	Remarks and references to Appendices
VILLERS BRULIN	24.3.17	Routine as usual. Arrangements made to evacuate to maximum 9 tured asked for. Foundling horse issued to 22nd A.G. 14 Cases admitted. WB	
	28.3.17	65. Animals transferred sick to No 22 Vet Hosp. One Horse left on route & later destroyed & buried, Mule destroyed & skinned 4 hides sent to 22nd Vet Hosp. WB	
	29.3.17	Routine as usual. WB	
	30.3.17	Routine as usual. Conducting party reported Y. P.M. WB	
	31.3.17	Routine as usual. 5 Cases admitted. W Bainbridge/Capt O.C. 44 MVS.	

(73989) W4141—463. 400,000. 9/14. H.&J.Ltd. Forms/C. 2118/10.

CONFIDENTIAL

WAR DIARY

OF

44ᵀᴴ MOBILE VETERINARY SECTION

34ᵀᴴ DIVISION

FROM APRIL 1ˢᵀ TO APRIL 30ᵀᴴ 1917

Army Form C. 2118.

WAR DIARY
or
INTELLIGENCE SUMMARY.
(Erase heading not required.)

Instructions regarding War Diaries and Intelligence Summaries are contained in F.S. Regs., Part II. and the Staff Manual respectively. Title pages will be prepared in manuscript.

Hour, Date, Place	Summary of Events and Information	Remarks and references to Appendices
VILLERS BRULIN 1.4.19.	Routine changed to that for Summer. 36 Cases admitted. WB.	
2.4.19	Routine as usual. 122 Cases admitted. WB.	
3.4.19	Routine as usual. 4 & 2 Horses destroyed. Party Rpt from 78th Brigade. 9.14th D.A.C. owing to their being 198 animals in Hospital. 24 Cases admitted. WB.	
4.4.19	Routine as usual. S.S. Sigley & Nowby Trans Sect to No 6. Stationery Hospital. 145 animals transferred sect to No 22 Vet. Hospital from TINQUES. 7 Horses destroyed. All carcases buried. 7 Sections sent to Base. Section moved from VILLERS BRULIN. to AGNIERES & billeted there arriving at 9 P.M. 16. Drs RFA. sent to Base with H Section men as conducting party. WB.	
AGNIERES 5.4.19	Routine as usual. WB.	
6.4.19.	Routine as usual. Orders to establish Advanced Collecting Post on Br.. 58 Cases admitted. WB.	

WAR DIARY or INTELLIGENCE SUMMARY

Army Form C. 2118.

Hour, Date, Place	Summary of Events and Information	Remarks and references to Appendices
AGNIERES 7.4.19	50 Cases transferred sick to No 22 Vet. Hosp. from A.V.S./GH.Q. Station. Party of 4 Drivers RFA. kept as Section by arrangement. Cpl Gent reported from conducting party. 39 Cases admitted. WyB.	
" 8.4.19	Routine as usual. Advanced collecting post established at appointed place consisting of 1 NCO & 1 Pte. 52 Cases admitted. WyB.	
" 9.4.19	48 Cases transferred sick from Aubigny Station to No 22 Vet. Hosp. 3 men borrowed from 21 M.V.S. to act as conducting party. Post relieved. 2 animals brought to Section & admitted. 4 br. RFA returned to Unit. Cpl Dexter reported from conducting party reported Pte Crabtree absent, however arrested by M.M.P. in ABBEVILLE. 43 more cases admitted. WyB.	
" 10.4.19	Routine as usual. ADVS visited Section. 11 Cases admitted. WyB.	
" 11.4.19	Routine as usual. Pte Power reported sick & Collecting Post relieved. 6 Horses buried. Conducting party reported. 3 men returned to 21st MVS. WyB.	
" 12.4.19	Routine as usual. 15 Cases admitted. WyB.	

WAR DIARY
or
INTELLIGENCE SUMMARY.
(Erase heading not required.)

Army Form C. 2118.

Hour, Date, Place	Summary of Events and Information	Remarks and references to Appendices
AGMERES. 13. 4. 14.	Routine as usual. Arrangements made for 20 P.B. men to report at Section for gravel digging to-morrow. 10 Cases admitted	WyB.
" 14. 4. 14	19 Cases evacuated sick from AUBIGNY station. Gun conducting party. Corpl Gent i/c. who was instructed to bring back Pte Crabtree from A.P.M. ABBEVILLE 53rd M.V.S. (63rd RN Division arrived at Section at 2 P.M. to take over. Section to move on relief to CHELERS collecting but received & arrangements made to move to-morrow. 20 P.B. men reported for grave digging. 30 Cases admitted	WyB.
" 15. 4. 14	32 Cases handed over to 53rd M.V.S. also bells and stabling Section moved off 10.30 P.M. & proceeded to CHELERS & billeted there	WyB.
CHELERS 16. 4. 14.	Routine as usual. Corpl Gent reported from conducting party. also Pte Crabtree under escort.	WyB.
" 19. 4. 14.	Routine as usual Pte Crabtree brought to Orderly Room & crabs read Orders to collect there from. ESTREVILLE. Annual found dead on arrival S.R.M brought to Section 1. Case admitted	WyB.
" 31. 4. 14	Routine as usual. 12. Cases admitted	WyB.

WAR DIARY
or
INTELLIGENCE SUMMARY.

(Erase heading not required.)

Army Form C. 2118.

Hour, Date, Place		Summary of Events and Information	Remarks and references to Appendices
CHELERS	19. 4. 17	16 Cases evacuated from TINQUES to No 22 Vet Hosp. Orders received to move on 21st. Went to TILLOY-LES-HERMAVILLE & arranged billets. 5 Cases admitted. WyB.	
"	20. 4. 17	Routine as usual. Parade for pay. 60 blankets obtained to 19.9.9.0.S. Parade for inspection & cutting down kit. Arrangements made to move tomorrow. WyB.	
"	21. 4. 17	Moved off from CHELERS 10.30 A.M. & arrived at TILLOY-LES-HERMAVILLE 12.45 P.M. 1 billeted. Reported in person to A.D.V.S. WyB.	
TILLOY LES HERMAVILLE	22. 4. 17	Routine as usual. 2 Cases admitted WyB.	
"	23. 4. 17	Routine as usual. Route to new advanced dressing Post reconnoitred in company with A.D.V.S. also section of 57 3/3 Div on ACQ. Received orders to move tomorrow to LARRESSET. Arrangement made with Town Major of their camp for accommodation. 2 Cases admitted. WyB.	
"	24. 4. 17	Parade 10.15 A.M. & moved off from TILLOY-LES-HERMAVILLE to LARRESSET & billeted WyB.	

Army Form C. 2118

WAR DIARY
or
INTELLIGENCE SUMMARY
(Erase heading not required.)

Instructions regarding War Diaries and Intelligence Summaries are contained in F.S. Regs., Part II. and the Staff Manual respectively. Title Pages will be prepared in manuscript.

Place	Date	Hour	Summary of Events and Information	Remarks and references to Appendices
LARRESSET	25.4.17		Routine as usual. Advanced Collecting & Dressing Post taken over from 61 Division at FEBRUARY CIRCUS. ST NICHOLAS. consisting of 1 Corp. & 1 Cpl. 2 Cases admitted	WB.
"	26.4.17.		Routine as usual. Advanced Dressing Post visited. 3 Cases admitted	WB.
"	27.4.17.		Routine as usual. 1 Corp. & 10 men sent to FREVENT to collect 21 h.d Mules (Remounts) 1 Case admitted	WB.
"	28.4.17		21 Remounts taken to refilling point. 13 issued there & remainder sent to Advanced Dressing Post for collection by Units. 14 Cases admitted	WB.
"	29.4.17.		Routine as usual. Float sent to No 3 Sec D.A.C. for Mule. S.S. BELLINGER W. No 35.37. reported for duty from No 6 Vet Hosp. 16 Cases admitted	WB.
"	30.4.17.		Routine as usual. 2 Cases admitted. 41 Cases evacuated from AGNEZ to No 22 Vet Hosp.	WBainbridge Capt a.v.c. O.C 44 M.U.S.

1875 Wt. W593/826 1,000,000 4/15 J.B.C. & A. A.D.S.S./Forms/C.2118.

Confidential War Diary of 44th M.V.S 34th Division

From 1.5.19 to 31.5.19.

WAR DIARY
or
INTELLIGENCE SUMMARY

(Erase heading not required.)

Army Form C. 2118

Instructions regarding War Diaries and Intelligence Summaries are contained in F. S. Regs., Part II. and the Staff Manual respectively. Title Pages will be prepared in manuscript.

Place	Date	Hour	Summary of Events and Information	Remarks and references to Appendices
LARRESSET	1.5.14		Routine as usual. Orders received to remove Section to LE CAUROY tomorrow. One case transferred to M.V.S. 15th Division. WJB.	
	2.5.14		Reveille 4.30 A.M. Parade 7.45 A.M. & marched off. Arrived LE CAUROY 3.45 P.M. & billeted. WJB.	
LE CAUROY	3.5.14		Routine as usual. Cleaning up billets. WJB.	
	4.5.14		Routine as usual. Arrangements made with R.T.O. FREVANT to transfer sick animals from that station. 5 cases admitted. WJB.	
	5.5.14		Routine as usual. 6 cases admitted. WJB.	
	6.5.14		11 cases transferred sick from FREVANT to 22nd Veterinary Hospital. Conducting party ordered to report at BERNAVILLE. Section under orders to move tomorrow. All ranks sent to 103rd Infy Brigade Baths. WJB.	
	7.5.14		Reveille 4.30 A.M. Parade 7.30 A.M. Horse rugs handed in to Salvage through Town Major. Marched off 7.45 A.M. Arrived at BERNAVILLE 3.30 P.M. & billeted. WJB.	

Army Form C. 2118

WAR DIARY
or
INTELLIGENCE SUMMARY
(Erase heading not required.)

Instructions regarding War Diaries and Intelligence Summaries are contained in F. S. Regs., Part II. and the Staff Manual respectively. Title Pages will be prepared in manuscript.

Place	Date	Hour	Summary of Events and Information	Remarks and references to Appendices
BERNAYVILLE	8.5.17		Routine as usual. Pte's Macey & Owen reported from ABBEVILLE. WyD.	
"	9.5.17		Routine as usual. WyD.	
"	10.5.17		Routine as usual. Col. Dexter & Pte. Frank Charlton & Power inoculated. WyD.	
"	11.5.17		Routine as usual. 12 Remounts collected from DOULLENS at 5 A.M. 2 Cars admitted. WyD.	
"	12.5.17		Routine as usual. Parade for inspection. 2 Cars admitted. WyD.	
"	13.5.17		Routine as usual. A.A. & Q.M.G. inspected section with A.D.V.S. Remounts issued. 6 Cars admitted. WyD.	
"	14.5.17		Routine as usual. 1 Case admitted. WyD.	
"	15.5.17		Routine as usual. WyD.	

Army Form C. 2118

WAR DIARY
or
INTELLIGENCE SUMMARY
(Erase heading not required.)

Instructions regarding War Diaries and Intelligence Summaries are contained in F. S. Regs., Part II. and the Staff Manual respectively. Title Pages will be prepared in manuscript.

Place	Date	Hour	Summary of Events and Information	Remarks and references to Appendices
BERMAYILLE	16.5.17		Routine as usual	
"	17.5.17		Routine as usual.	
"	18.5.17		Routine as usual. Mule found straying by M.M.P. sent to Section. 3 horses admitted	
"	19.5.17		Routine as usual.	
"	20.5.17		Routine as usual. Pte Bishop granted leave to England	
"	21.5.17		14 horses transferred sick from CANDAS. to 22nd Veterinary Hospital ABBEVILLE	
"	22.5.17		Routine as usual.	
"	23.5.17		Collecting party reported. 23 Remounts collected from DOULLENS. & brought to Section	
"	24.5.17		Routine as usual. All Section sent to Divisional Baths	

1875 Wt. W593/826 1,000,000 4/15 J.B.C. & A. A.D.S.S./Forms/C. 2118.

Army Form C. 2118

WAR DIARY
or
INTELLIGENCE SUMMARY
(Erase heading not required.)

Instructions regarding War Diaries and Intelligence Summaries are contained in F. S. Regs., Part II. and the Staff Manual respectively. Title Pages will be prepared in manuscript.

Place	Date	Hour	Summary of Events and Information	Remarks and references to Appendices
BERNAVILLE	25.5.17		Routine as usual. Dr Nicholls granted leave to England. Parade for hay. 1 case admitted	WB.
"	26.5.17		Routine as usual. 1 case admitted	WB.
"	27.5.17		Routine as usual. Orders received to move on 29th inst under orders of G.O. 102nd Inf Bde. 1 case admitted	WB.
"	28.5.17		Routine as usual. 3 cases transferred from CANDAS to 22nd Veterinary Hospital ABBEVILLE	WB.
"	29.5.17	7.20 AM	Reveille 4.20 AM. Moved off from BERNAVILLE. M.O. Mare left with farmer at billet D.29 suffering from Laminitis. Arrived at COUTURELLE 4.20 PM. 1 killed	WB.
COUTURELLE	30.5.17		Reveille 5 AM. Parade 8 AM and moved off from COUTURELLE. Arrived at LARESSET & billeted.	WB.
LARESSET	31.5.17		Dr Mellor sent to 104th F Ambulance. Collecting boat established at 9.16 a.s.2. Dismount. Collected from AUBIGNY station & brought to section	

WBanniday
Capt A.V.C.
O.C. 44 M.V.S.

CONFIDENTIAL

WAR DIARY

OF

44TH MOBILE VETERINARY SECTION

34TH DIVISION

From June 1st 1914 to June 30th 1914.

Army Form C. 2118

WAR DIARY
or
INTELLIGENCE SUMMARY
(Erase heading not required.)

Instructions regarding War Diaries and Intelligence Summaries are contained in F. S. Regs., Part II. and the Staff Manual respectively. Title Pages will be prepared in manuscript.

Place	Date	Hour	Summary of Events and Information	Remarks and references to Appendices
LARESSET	1.6.19		Routine as usual. Site selected for camp at G.14.a. central. WB	
"	2.6.19.		Remounts issued. Arrangements made to move Section tomorrow. 5 Peters transferred from Section to 101st Inf Brigade. WB	
"	3.6.19		Reveille 5 a.m. Parade 7.45 a.m. Moved off from billet to G.14.a. central. bivouacked WB	
G.a.14 Central	4.6.19		Routine as usual. Cpls Gent & Ples Smith & Power tempory detached to b/o Horse Res. Camp for duty. 6 cases admitted WB	
"	5.6.19		Collecting post relieved and cases brought to Section. Arrangements made with F.S.O. & R.16. ARRAS to evacuate from that station tomorrow. Pte Bishop reported from leave. 4 cases admitted WB	
"	6.6.19		35 cases transferred sick from Arras to 22 Veterinary Hospital. Pte Woods reported sick with sprained ankle. 15 Saddles & bridles returned to salvage. 5 horses having been transferred on the 2nd inst. 4 cases admitted WB	
"	7.6.19		Collecting post called in. Site being taken over by MVS. 9th Division. One horse returned to duty. Dr Nicholls reported from leave. 7 cases admitted WB	

Army Form C. 2118

WAR DIARY
or
INTELLIGENCE SUMMARY
(Erase heading not required.)

Instructions regarding War Diaries and Intelligence Summaries are contained in F.S. Regs., Part II. and the Staff Manual respectively. Title Pages will be prepared in manuscript.

Place	Date	Hour	Summary of Events and Information	Remarks and references to Appendices
G.H.Q. cont.	8.6.14		Routine as usual. 13 cases admitted. WB	
...	9.6.14		Routine as usual. 1 case admitted. WB	
...	10.6.14		Routine as usual. Pte Paul reported sick. Parade for pay. 1 case admitted. WB	
...	11.6.14		Routine as usual. 31 cases transferred sick from Anzac to 22 Veterinary Hospital. Pte Paul admitted to 104th Field Ambulance suffering from Brights disease. 16 cases admitted. WB	
...	12.6.14		Routine as usual. 3 cases admitted. WB	
...	13.6.14		Routine as usual. 8 cases transferred sick from Anzac to 22nd Veterinary Hospital. 2 cases admitted. WB	
...	14.6.14		Routine as usual. 4 cases admitted. WB	
...	15.6.14		Routine as usual. Parade for inspection. 12 cases admitted. WB	
...	16.6.14		Routine as usual. 15 cases transferred sick from Anzac to 22 Vet Hospital. WB	

Army Form C. 2118

WAR DIARY
or
INTELLIGENCE SUMMARY
(Erase heading not required.)

Instructions regarding War Diaries and Intelligence Summaries are contained in F. S. Regs., Part II. and the Staff Manual respectively. Title Pages will be prepared in manuscript.

Place	Date	Hour	Summary of Events and Information	Remarks and references to Appendices
G.H.Q. Central	17.6.17		Routine as usual. No 534 Sgt Proctor A. promoted a/s/Sgt. Vide Local Corps Order.	
"	18.6.17		Routine as usual. Orders received to despatch Staff Sergt Proctor to 24 Vet. Hosp. on relief by another Sergt. Corp Cooper granted leave to England. 8 cases admitted.	
"	19.6.17		Routine as usual. 1 case admitted	
"	20.6.17		Routine as usual. 14 cases transferred sick from Anac to 22 Veterinary Hosp.	
"	21.6.17		Routine as usual. Arrangements made to move camp tomorrow.	
"	22.6.17		Parade 9 a.m. and moved off from camp. Leos 1 N.C.O. & 2 Geo left at Corps Horse Regt Camp. Arrived at TILLOY-LES-HERMAVILLE 12.45. Mans billeted	
TILLOY-LES HERMAVILLE	23.6.17		Routine as usual. Parade all ranks for pay. No T.O 2165 Sgt Taylor G. reported from H8th Division M.Y.S.	
"	24.6.17		Routine as usual. Staff Sergt Proctor despatched to No24 Veterinary Hospital Journey en Bray.	

Army Form C. 2118

WAR DIARY
or
INTELLIGENCE SUMMARY

(Erase heading not required.)

Instructions regarding War Diaries and Intelligence Summaries are contained in F. S. Regs., Part II. and the Staff Manual respectively. Title Pages will be prepared in manuscript.

Place	Date	Hour	Summary of Events and Information	Remarks and references to Appendices
TILLOY-LES-HERMAVILLE	25.6.17		Routine as usual. Col Tyler. A.A. & Q.M.G. 34th Div: inspected section billets, cook-house etc.	
"	26.6.17		Routine as usual.	
"	27.6.17		Routine as usual.	
"	28.6.17		Routine as usual. Ptes Strond & Crabtree granted leave to England. 2 cases admitted.	
"	29.6.17		Routine as usual. Parade for inspection of Rifles, drill, Kit and gas helmet drill. 4 cases admitted.	
"	30.6.17		Routine as usual.	

WBambridge
Capt. a.v.c
O.C. 44 M.V.S.

Vol 19

CONFIDENTIAL

WAR DIARY

OF

44ᵀᴴ M.V.S.

34ᵀᴴ DIVISION

FROM

JULY 1ˢᵗ 1917 TO JULY 31ˢᵀ 1917

Army Form C. 2118

WAR DIARY
or
INTELLIGENCE SUMMARY
(Erase heading not required.)

Instructions regarding War Diaries and Intelligence Summaries are contained in F.S. Regs., Part II. and the Staff Manual respectively. Title Pages will be prepared in manuscript.

Place	Date	Hour	Summary of Events and Information	Remarks and references to Appendices
VILLOY-LES-ERMAYVILLE	1.4.19		Routine as usual. No 10160 A/Corp Cooper reported from leave. 5 cases admitted	WB
"	2.4.19		Routine as usual. No 21426 Pte Gang W. joined unit from No.1 Veterinary Hospital 2 cases admitted	WB
"	3.4.19		Routine as usual. Arrangements made to evacuate sick animals to morrow. Cpl. Gent and 2 Ptes rejoined Unit from Base Area Rest Camp. 5 cases admitted	WB
"	4.4.19		23 Sick animals trans ferred sick from AUBIGNY Station to No 22 Veterinary Hospital	WB
"	5.4.19		Routine as usual. Orders received to proceed with Section to LIGNY station to entrain for PERONNE tomorrow.	WB
"	6.4.19		Reveille 2.a.m. Marched off from billets 3 AM. Arrived LIGNY STATION 5.30 a.m. Entrained Horses & Waggons and left LIGNY 9.a.m. Arrived at PERONNE 5.15 P.M. detrained and marched to camp & bivouacked 6.25 P.M.	WB

1875 Wt. W593/826 1,000,000 4/15 J.B.C. & A. A.D.S.S./Forms/C. 2118.

Army Form C. 2118

WAR DIARY
or
INTELLIGENCE SUMMARY

(Erase heading not required.)

Instructions regarding War Diaries and Intelligence Summaries are contained in F. S. Regs., Part II. and the Staff Manual respectively. Title Pages will be prepared in manuscript.

Place	Date	Hour	Summary of Events and Information	Remarks and references to Appendices
QUINCONCE	7.7.17		Routine as usual. 1 sheel of float broken. 1 casualty reported. MyB.	
"	8.7.17		Routine as usual. 1 N.C.O. and 4 men sent to Abbeville to bring back 16 Remounts. MyB.	
"	9.7.17		Routine as usual. Received at 10.30 am to proceed to G.2.2. Cent. M.9p.62.c. left Camp 3.30 PM & arrived G.2.2.c. 6 PM. Float left at 4 Light Mobile Workshops PERONNE MyB.	
G.2.2. Cent.	10.7.17		Routine as usual. MyB.	
"	11.7.17		Routine as usual. Geo. Grant & Crabtree reported from leave. No 2391 joined Unit from No 22 Veterinary Hosp. 11 Cases admitted. MyB.	
"	12.7.17		Routine as usual. 16 Remounts received from ABBEVILLE. 6 Cases admitted. MyB.	
"	13.7.17		Routine as usual. Orders received to detach 1 N.C.O., 3 Ptes. to III Corps Mobile Veterinary Detachment also 1 Rider. Completion reported. 16 Cases admitted. MyB.	
"	14.7.17		32 Cases transferred out to No1 Veterinary Hosp. FORGES-LES-EAUX from Rail Station. Remounts issued. MyB.	

Army Form C. 2118

WAR DIARY
or
INTELLIGENCE SUMMARY
(Erase heading not required.)

Instructions regarding War Diaries and Intelligence Summaries are contained in F.S. Regs., Part II. and the Staff Manual respectively. Title Pages will be prepared in manuscript.

Place	Date	Hour	Summary of Events and Information	Remarks and references to Appendices
G.22.cent	15.7.17		Routine as usual. WB.	
"	16.7.17		Routine as usual. Ptes Duff & Ellis granted leave to England. No 21426 Pte Fanny admitted to No 5. Casualty Clearing Station from detached duty at III Corps Mobile Veterinary Detachment. WB.	
"	17.7.17		Routine as usual. Pte Williams granted leave to England. 14 Cases admitted. WB.	
"	18.7.17		Routine as usual. Pte Smith granted leave to England. WB.	
"	19.7.17		Routine as usual. Pte Owen granted leave to England. 1 Case admitted. WB.	
"	20.7.17		Routine as usual. Corp Cooper sent to Corps Mobile Veterinary Detachment to replace Sergt Gent. Pte Turnbull granted leave to England. 9 cases admitted. WB.	
"	21.7.17		22 Cases transferred sick from NOISEL STATION to No7 Veterinary Hosp. FORGES-LES-EAUX. 2 Cases admitted. WB.	
"	22.7.17		Routine as usual. WB.	

Army Form C. 2118

WAR DIARY
or
INTELLIGENCE SUMMARY

(Erase heading not required.)

Instructions regarding War Diaries and Intelligence Summaries are contained in F. S. Regs., Part II. and the Staff Manual respectively. Title Pages will be prepared in manuscript.

Place	Date	Hour	Summary of Events and Information	Remarks and references to Appendices
G.22 cent.	23.7.17		Routine as usual. 1,000 francs drawn from Field Cashier. 2 cases admitted	
"	24.7.17		Routine as usual	
"	25.7.17		Routine as usual	
"	26.7.17		Routine as usual. 3 cases admitted	
"	27.7.17		Routine as usual. Pte. Ellis & Pte. Duff reported back from leave. Pte. Bright granted leave. Parade all ranks for pay. 3 cases admitted	
LES-F AUX	28.7.17		Routine as usual. 5 animals transferred sick to No 1 Vet. Hospital FORGES. Pte Williams reported back from leave	
"	29.7.17		Routine as usual. Pte Smith reported back from leave	
"	30.7.17		Routine as usual. Pte Owen back from leave. Pte Wills from evacuation. Case admitted	
"	31.7.17		Routine as usual	

W.J. Bainbridge, Capt. A.V.C.
O.C. 44 Mobile Veterinary Section

1875. Wt. W593/826 1,000,000 4/15 J.B.C. & A. A.D.S.S./Forms/C. 2118.

CONFIDENTIAL
WAR DIARY.
OF
44th MOBILE VETERINARY SECTION
34th DIVISION

FROM 1st AUGUST 1917 TO 31st AUGUST 1917

WAR DIARY or INTELLIGENCE SUMMARY

Army Form C. 2118

Place	Date	Hour	Summary of Events and Information	Remarks and references to Appendices
Sheet 62 c. R.22.c.	1.8.17		Routine as usual. 1 case admitted. WB.	
"	2.8.17		Routine as usual. 17 Foundlings received. 1 case admitted. WB.	
"	3.8.17		Routine as usual. Pte Turnbull reported back from leave to England. Arrangements made with D.S.O. ROISEL for evacuation of sick animals to morrow. 9 cases admitted. WB.	
"	4.8.17		Routine as usual. 17 animals transferred sick from ROISEL station to FORGES-LES-EAUX. Pte Ward (707648) joined from No.3 Veterinary Hospital. 1 case admitted. WB.	
"	5.8.17		Routine as usual. Pte Owen sent to III Corps Mob: Vet Detachment for duty. 3 cases admitted. WB.	
"	6.8.17		Routine as usual. 1 case admitted. WB.	
"	7.8.17		Routine as usual. Evacuation party reported back from Forges to Eaux. Parade for Gas Helmet Drill. 2 cases admitted. WB.	
"	8.8.17		Routine as usual. No.12319 Pte Woods granted leave to England. No.14368 Pte Bright reported back from leave. WB.	

WAR DIARY
or
INTELLIGENCE SUMMARY
(Erase heading not required.)

Army Form C. 2118

Place	Date	Hour	Summary of Events and Information	Remarks and references to Appendices
R.22.C	9.5.17		Routine as usual. 8 cases admitted. MB.	
"	10.5.17		Routine as usual. Arrangements made with R.J.O. Roisel station for evacuation of sick animals tomorrow. 8 cases admitted. MB.	
"	11.5.17		Routine as usual. 16 sick animals transferred from Roisel to No 7 Veterinary Hospital Forges-les-Eaux. MB.	
"	12.5.17		Routine as usual. Staff Sergt Harper, S.S. Bellinger, Ptes Will, Kirk & Stuart granted leave to England. 2 Surplus animals received from R.E. MB.	
"	13.5.17		Routine as usual. 3 cases admitted. MB.	
"	14.5.17		Routine as usual. Conducting party reported back from Forges les Eaux. 2 cases admitted. Pte Jobling granted leave to England. MB.	
"	15.5.17		Routine as usual. 1 case admitted. MB.	
"	16.5.17		Routine as usual. 1 case admitted. MB.	
"	17.5.17		Routine as usual. Arrangements made with R.J.O. Roisel for evacuation of sick animals tomorrow. 9 cases admitted. MB.	

Army Form C. 2118

WAR DIARY
or
INTELLIGENCE SUMMARY
(Erase heading not required.)

Instructions regarding War Diaries and Intelligence Summaries are contained in F.S. Regs., Part II. and the Staff Manual respectively. Title Pages will be prepared in manuscript.

Place	Date	Hour	Summary of Events and Information	Remarks and references to Appendices
K.22.C.	18.8.14		Routine as usual. 12 animals transferred sick from No.1 Sec. to No.1 Veterinary Hospital. Forges les Eaux. 1 case admitted. WB.	
...	19.8.14		Routine as usual. WB.	
...	20.8.14		Routine as usual. Conducting party reported back from Forges les Eaux. WB.	
...	21.8.14		Routine as usual. Pte Woods reported from leave. WB.	
...	22.8.14		Routine as usual. 4 cases admitted. WB.	
...	23.8.14		Routine as usual. 2 cases admitted. WB.	
...	24.8.14		Routine as usual. Arrangements made with C.H.O. Rouen for evacuation of sick animals to morrow. WB.	
...	25.8.14		Routine as usual. 10 cases transferred sick from No.1 Sec. to No.1 Veterinary Hospital - Forges les Eaux. Staff Sergt Harper S.S. Bellinger & Pte Willis left & Pte Wood granted leave to England. WB.	
...	26.8.14		Routine as usual. ADVS visited section. WB.	
...	27.8.14		Routine as usual. Dr Topping back from leave. Conducting party reported from Forges les Eaux. 1 case admitted. WB.	

1875 Wt. W593/826 1,000,000 4/15 J.B.C. & A. A.D.S.S./Forms/C. 2118.

Army Form C. 2118

WAR DIARY
or
INTELLIGENCE SUMMARY

(Erase heading not required.)

Instructions regarding War Diaries and Intelligence Summaries are contained in F. S. Regs., Part II. and the Staff Manual respectively. Title Pages will be prepared in manuscript.

Place	Date	Hour	Summary of Events and Information	Remarks and references to Appendices
R.22.c.	28.8.14		Routine as usual. 1 case admitted. WB.	
...	29.8.14		Routine as usual. Inspection of Rifles & Equipment. Gas Helmet drill. WB	
...	30.8.14		Routine as usual. DDVS Inspected Section. WB	
...	31.8.14		Routine as usual. 3 Float cases fetched. Arrangements made with PVO. Orders for evacuation of sick Animals to morrow. 19 Cases admitted.	

T.W.Bainbridge/Capt A.V.C
O.C. 44 Mob. Vet. Sect.

CONFIDENTIAL

WAR DIARY

OF

44ᵀᴴ MOBILE VETERINARY SECTION 34ᵀᴴ DIVISION

FROM SEPT 1ˢᵗ 1917 TO SEPT 30ᵀᴴ 1917.

Army Form C. 2118

WAR DIARY
or
INTELLIGENCE SUMMARY

(Erase heading not required.)

Instructions regarding War Diaries and Intelligence Summaries are contained in F. S. Regs., Part II. and the Staff Manual respectively. Title Pages will be prepared in manuscript.

Place	Date	Hour	Summary of Events and Information	Remarks and references to Appendices
Sheet 62c. K.22.c.	1.9.17		Routine as usual. 27 animals transferred sick from ROISEL to No.7 Veterinary Hospital FORGES-LES-EAUX. WB.	
" "	2.9.17		Routine as usual 4 cases admitted. WB.	
" "	3.9.17		Routine as usual. Arrangements made with R.T.O. ROISEL for evacuation of sick animals to morrow 8 cases admitted. WB.	
" "	4.9.17		Routine as usual. 12 animals transferred sick from ROISEL to No.7 Veterinary Hospital FORGES-LES-EAUX. Conducting party reported back 3 cases admitted. WB.	
" "	5.9.17		Routine as usual. WB.	
" "	6.9.17		Routine as usual. Conducting party reported back. Rifle and Gas Helmet drill. 2 cases admitted. WB.	
" "	7.9.17		Routine as usual. Parade all ranks for pay. No 7648 Pte Ward reported back from leave. Arrangements made with R.T.O. ROISEL for evacuation of sick animals to morrow. 15 cases admitted. WB.	

Army Form C. 2118

WAR DIARY
or
INTELLIGENCE SUMMARY

(Erase heading not required.)

Instructions regarding War Diaries and Intelligence Summaries are contained in F. S. Regs., Part II. and the Staff Manual respectively. Title Pages will be prepared in manuscript.

Place	Date	Hour	Summary of Events and Information	Remarks and references to Appendices
Sheet 62 c. R 22.c	8.9.17		Routine as usual. 18 animals transferred sick from ROISEL to No7 Veterinary Hospital FORGES-LES-EAUX. 2 cases admitted	WB.
"	9.9.17		Routine as usual. No.117,02,165 Sergt Taylor.A. granted leave to England.	WB.
"	10.9.17		Routine as usual. Arrangements made with R.T.O. ROISEL for evacuation of sick animals to morrow. No 11892 Corp Dexter M. granted leave to SENS. 16 animals cast by DDR III Corp received at section. 14 cases admitted. Conducting party reported back.	WB.
"	11.9.17		Routine as usual. 32 cases transferred from ROISEL to No7 Veterinary Hospital. 3 cases admitted.	WB.
"	12.9.17		Routine as usual. 2 cases admitted.	WB.
"	13.9.17		Routine as usual. Conducting party reported back.	WB.
"	14.9.17		Routine as usual. Arrangements made with R.T.O. ROISEL for evacuation of sick animals to morrow. 26 cases admitted. Received orders to move to VRAIGNES to-morrow.	WB.
"	15.9.17		Routine as usual. 32 cases transferred sick from ROISEL to No7 Veterinary Hosp. FORGES-LES-EAUX. Moved off from Camp 12.45 P.M. Arrived at VRAIGNES 2 P.M. 7 Billeted	WB.

WAR DIARY or INTELLIGENCE SUMMARY

Army Form C. 2118

Place	Date	Hour	Summary of Events and Information	Remarks and references to Appendices
FRAIGNES	16.9.17		Routine as usual. 8 cases admitted. WB.	
"	17.9.17		Routine as usual. Arrangements made with R.T.O. ROISEL for evacuation of sick animals to mornal. 17 cases admitted. WB.	
"	18.9.17		2.3. cases transferred sick from ROISEL to No. 7 Veterinary Hospital FORGES-LES-EAUX. WB.	
"	19.9.17		Routine as usual. Conducting party reported back. 1 case admitted. WB.	
"	20.9.17		Routine as usual. 2 cases admitted. WB.	
"	21.9.17		Routine as usual. 17 animals cast by D.P.R.II. Cofs received at Section. Arrangements made with R.T.O. ROISEL for evacuation of such animals to mornal. 17 cases admitted. Conask all ranks for cofs. WB.	
"	22.9.17		64 animals (including 17 cast animals) transferred from ROISEL to No. 7 Veterinary Hosp: FORGES-LES-EAUX. No. T/02165 Sgt Taylor A. reported from leave. No. 11892 Cofs Dexter A. reported back from leave. WB.	
"	23.9.17		Routine as usual. Conducting party reported back. WB.	
"	24.9.17		Routine as usual. Arrangements made with R.T.O. ROISEL for evacuation of sick animals to mornal. 21 cases admitted. WB.	

Army Form C. 2118

WAR DIARY
or
INTELLIGENCE SUMMARY
(Erase heading not required.)

Instructions regarding War Diaries and Intelligence Summaries are contained in F. S. Regs., Part II. and the Staff Manual respectively. Title Pages will be prepared in manuscript.

Place	Date	Hour	Summary of Events and Information	Remarks and references to Appendices
VRAIGNES	25.9.17		2 H animals transferred sick from ROISEL to No 7 Veterinary Hospital FORGES-LES-EAUX.	WB
"	26.9.17		Routine as usual. No H 527 Sgt Gent J.R. granted leave to England	WB
"	27.9.17		Routine as usual. ADVS inspected Section	WB
"	28.9.17		Routine as usual. Received orders to hand over billets to 36 MVS & proceed with Section to PERONNE to-morrow	WB
"	29.9.17		Reveille 6.30 A.M. Parade 9.15 A.M. Marched off 9.30 A.M. arrived at PERONNE 11.30 A.M. & billeted	WB
PERONNE	30.9.17		Reveille 5 A.M. Parade 7.5 A.M Marched off 7.10 A.M arrived at BAPAUME 12.20 P.M & camped.	

WBambridge Capt A.V.C
O.C. 44 M.tt. V.t. Sect.

CONFIDENTIAL

WAR DIARY.
OF
44 M.V.S
34 DIVISION
FROM
OCT 1st 1917. TO OCT 31st 1917

Army Form C. 2118

WAR DIARY
or
INTELLIGENCE SUMMARY
(Erase heading not required.)

Instructions regarding War Diaries and Intelligence Summaries are contained in F. S. Regs., Part II. and the Staff Manual respectively. Title Pages will be prepared in manuscript.

Place	Date	Hour	Summary of Events and Information	Remarks and references to Appendices
BAPAUME	1.10.17		Reveille 5.15 A.M. Parade 7.15 A.M. Marched off 7.20 A.M. arrived at BASSEUX 11.20 P.M. and billeted. WB	
BASSEUX	2.10.17		Routine as usual. WB	
"	3.10.17		Routine as usual. 7. Cases admitted. WB	
"	4.10.17		Routine as usual. 9. Cases admitted. WB	
"	5.10.17		Routine as usual. Arrangement made with 16. BEAUMETZ station for evacuation of sick animals to-morrow. Gas Helmet drill & rifle Inspection. Parade all ranks for pay: No 100040 Pte Power granted leave. WB	
"	6.10.17		Routine as usual. 16 animals transferred sick from BEAUMETZ to No7 Veterinary Hospital FORGES-LES-EAUX. Orders received to move to PROVEN. BELGIUM to-morrow. WB	
"	7.10.17		Routine as usual. Parade midnight and marched to BEAUMETZ station. WB	
"	8.10.17		Arrived BEAUMETZ 12.50 A.M. & entrained. Left BEAUMETZ 11.20 A.M. arrived at PROVEN 10.50 P.M. and billeted. WB	

Army Form C. 2118

WAR DIARY
or
INTELLIGENCE SUMMARY
(Erase heading not required.)

Place	Date	Hour	Summary of Events and Information	Remarks and references to Appendices
PROVEN	9.10.17		Routine as usual. 1 case admitted. WB	
"	10.10.17		Routine as usual. 1 N.C.O. and 3 men sent on Detachment duty to 14 Corps Veterinary Casualty Clearing Station. 4 cases admitted. WB	
"	11.10.17		Routine as usual. WB	
"	12.10.17		Routine as usual. Sgt Gent reported back from leave, and sent to relieve Cpl Cooper at Corps Casualty Clearing Station. 4 cases admitted. WB	
"	13.10.17		Routine as usual. 7 cases transferred sick to 14 Corps Veterinary Casualty Clearing Station. 8 men (Category B) joined to relieve (8 men Category A) Received orders to move forward from No 5 Veterinary Hospital area tomorrow. 1 N.C.O & 2 men took over Advanced Collecting Post at Gt & Lt Crabtee & Swn. relieved by Pte Henry & Arthington at C.C.S. WB	
"	14.10.17		Reveille 5.30 AM Parade 9.15 AM Marched off 9.30 AM. Arrived at A.Q.C.7.5 (Sheet 28) 10.30 AM and camped. A.D.V.S. visited section. 13 cases admitted WB	
A.Q.C.7.5	15.10.17		Routine as usual. A.D.V.S. visited Section. Moved to new camp at A.16.a.cent. 4 men (Category A) transferred to No 2 Vet. Hosp. 24 cases admitted. WB	

WAR DIARY or INTELLIGENCE SUMMARY

Army Form C. 2118

Place	Date	Hour	Summary of Events and Information	Remarks and references to Appendices
A.16.a.cent	16.10.17		Routine as usual. 32 cases admitted. WB.	
" "	17.10.17		Routine as usual. Orders received to move tomorrow to A.20.a.22 (Sheet 28) and form 14th Corps Veterinary Clearing Station. WB.	
A.20.a.22	18.10.17		Routine as usual. Section moved back to new camp. Advanced Post relieved. 9 cases admitted. WB.	
"	19.10.17		Routine as usual. Float at 14th Corps Casualty Clearing Station PROVEN for day. A.D.V.S. visited Section. 54 cases admitted. WB.	
"	20.10.17		Routine as usual. No 1007D Pte Power (Category A) transferred to No 2 Ver. Hospital. Water troughs erected. 43 cases admitted. WB.	
"	21.10.17		Routine as usual. 26 men reported from Mobile Veterinary Detachment with stores. Stores carried between M.V. & M.V.S. WB.	
"	22.10.17		Routine as usual. 50 Debility cases transferred sick to ST. OMER by road. D.A.D.V.S. visited section. Float lent to 17th Divl M.V.S. Men of M.V.S. divided. 81 cases admitted. WB.	
"	23.10.17		Arrangement made with R.T.O. International Corner Station for evacuation of sick animals tomorrow. Also with Ordnance Officer. WB.	

WAR DIARY
or
INTELLIGENCE SUMMARY
(Erase heading not required.)

Army Form C. 2118

Place	Date	Hour	Summary of Events and Information	Remarks and references to Appendices
A 20.a.22	23.10.17 (Cont.)		Swiss Cottage for empty carriage horses. Watering purposes on train & with R.T.O. for forage for animals & rations for conducting party. 20. Cases transferred sick by road to St OMERS. 11 Cases admitted. MJB	
"	24.10.17		8 Men reported from M.V.S. for conducting party. 247 animals transferred sick from INTERNATIONAL CORNER Station to No 13 Vet Hosp NEUFCHATEL. 2 19 V.S. visited section. 50 cases admitted. MJB	
"	25.10.17		30 animals evacuated to No 4 M.V.S. 102 cases admitted. MJB	
"	26.10.17		Routine as usual. 53 cases admitted. Arrangements made for evacuation of animals to morrow. Float lent to 29 M.V.S. for day. MJB	
"	27.10.17		Routine as usual. 133 Cases admitted. 199 cases transferred sick from INTERNATIONAL CORNER Station to No 13 Vet Hosp NEUFCHATEL. MJB	
"	28.10.17		Routine as usual. Received order to hand over to 2/1 West Lancs M.V.S. & proceed with Section to ACHIET-LE-PETIT to morrow. MJB	
"	29.10.17		Reveille 4 A.M. Marched off 6.15 A.M. arrived at PESELHOEK station 5.40 A.M. entrained 9.15 A.M. Arrived MIRAMONT 9.15 P.M. detrained and marched to ACHIET LE PETIT. Arrived 10.30 P.M. & BILLETED. MJB	

Army Form C. 2118

WAR DIARY
or
INTELLIGENCE SUMMARY
(Erase heading not required.)

Instructions regarding War Diaries and Intelligence Summaries are contained in F. S. Regs., Part II. and the Staff Manual respectively. Title Pages will be prepared in manuscript.

Place	Date	Hour	Summary of Events and Information	Remarks and references to Appendices
ACHIET-LE-PETIT.	30.10.17		Reveille 7 A.M. Parade 10 A.M. & marched off to new billets at BOISLEUX-AU-MONT arriving 1.15 P.M & billeted.	
BOISLEAUX-AU-MONT.	31.10.17		Routine as usual.	

W Bainbridge / Capt A.S.C.
O.C. 44 M.T.S.

CONFIDENTIAL

WAR DIARY
OF
44TH M.V.S.
34TH DIVISION
FROM
1.11.17 to 30.11.17

Army Form C. 2118

WAR DIARY
or
INTELLIGENCE SUMMARY
(Erase heading not required.)

Instructions regarding War Diaries and Intelligence Summaries are contained in F.S. Regs., Part II. and the Staff Manual respectively. Title Pages will be prepared in manuscript.

Place	Date	Hour	Summary of Events and Information	Remarks and references to Appendices
BOISLEUX AU-MONT	1.11.17		Routine as usual. 4 cases admitted. WB.	
"	2.11.17		Routine as usual. Carried on work building Stables. 14 cases admitted. WB.	
"	3.11.17		Routine as usual. Commenced clipping. Horse rugs drawn from Stores. 1 case admitted. WB.	
"	4.11.17		Routine as usual. Lecture on fitting saddlery and points of Horse given to new men. Arrangements made with R.V.O. BOISLEUX-AU-MONT for evacuation to-morrow. 3 cases admitted. WB.	
"	5.11.17		Routine as usual 16 animals transferred sick from BOISLEUX-AU-MONT to No 7 Veterinary Hospital. Forge les Eaux. 1 case admitted. WB.	
"	6.11.17		Routine as usual. Parade all ranks for Gas helmet drill & Inspection of Equipment and clothing. Rifle drill for new men. 12 cases admitted. WB.	
"	7.11.17		Routine as usual. Rifle drill for new men. Conducting party reported back. 2 cases admitted. WB.	

Army Form C. 2118

WAR DIARY
or
INTELLIGENCE SUMMARY
(Erase heading not required.)

Instructions regarding War Diaries and Intelligence Summaries are contained in F. S. Regs., Part II. and the Staff Manual respectively. Title Pages will be prepared in manuscript.

Place	Date	Hour	Summary of Events and Information	Remarks and references to Appendices
BOISLEUX AU-MONT	8.11.17		Routine as usual. Rifle drill for new men. Arrangements made with R.V.O. BOISLEUX-AU-MONT for evacuation to-morrow. 3 cases admitted. MWB	
"	9.11.17		Routine as usual. 24 Animals transferred sick from BOISLEUX-AU-MONT to No.7 Veterinary Hospital FORGES-LES-EAUX. MWB	
"	10.11.17		Routine as usual. 3 cases admitted MWB	
"	11.11.17		Routine as usual. No.31027 Pte Merry reported sick, conducting party reported back. 4 cases admitted MWB	
"	12.11.17		Routine as usual. No.31027 Pte Merry admitted to 104th Fd Ambulance 10 cases admitted MWB	
"	13.11.17		Routine as usual. Arrangements made with R.V.O. BOISLEUX-AU-MONT for evacuation of sick animals to-morrow. 9 cases admitted MWB	
"	14.11.17		Routine as usual. 18 animals transferred sick to No.7 Veterinary Hosp: FORGES-LES-EAUX from BOISLEUX-AU-MONT. 13 cases admitted MWB	
"	15.11.17		Riding drill for last joined men. 6 cases admitted MWB	
"	16.11.17		Riding drill for last joined men. 4 cases admitted No.11814 Pte Branks granted leave to Edg. MWB	

Army Form C. 2118

WAR DIARY
or
INTELLIGENCE SUMMARY

(Erase heading not required.)

Instructions regarding War Diaries and Intelligence Summaries are contained in F.S. Regs., Part II. and the Staff Manual respectively. Title Pages will be prepared in manuscript.

Place	Date	Hour	Summary of Events and Information	Remarks and references to Appendices
BOISLEUX-AU-MONT	17.11.17		Routine as usual. 1 case admitted. MWB	
"	18.11.17		Riding drill for men last joined. Arrangements made with R./S.C. BOISLEUX-AU-MONT for Evacuation of sick animals to-morrow. 3 cases admitted. MWB	
"	19.11.17		Routine as usual. 21 cases transferred sick from BOISLEUX-AU-MONT. to No. 7 Veterinary Hospital FORGES-LES-EAUX. 1 case admitted. MWB	
"	20.11.17		Routine as usual. 4 cases admitted. MWB	
"	21.11.17		Routine as usual. No. 3384 Pte Sturch reported sick and admitted to Hosp¹. Conducting party reported back. 6 cases admitted. MWB	
"	22.11.17		Routine as usual. Gas Helmet drill & Inspection of Equipment. Arrangements made with R./S.C. BOISLEUX-AU-MONT. for Evacuation of sick animals to-morrow. 4 cases admitted. MWB	
"	23.11.17		Routine as usual. 14 animals transferred sick from BOISLEUX-AU-MONT. to No. 7 Veterinary Hospital FORGES-LES-EAUX. 1 case admitted. MWB	
"	24.11.17		Routine as usual. 2 cases admitted. MWB	
"	25.11.17		Routine as usual. Conducting party reported back. 3 cases admitted. MWB	

WAR DIARY or INTELLIGENCE SUMMARY

Army Form C. 2118

Place	Date	Hour	Summary of Events and Information	Remarks and references to Appendices
BOISLEUX-AU-MONT	26.11.17		Routine as usual. 8 cases admitted. MWB	
"	27.11.17		Routine as usual. Arrangements made with R.O.I.C. BOISLEUX-AU-MONT for evacuation of sick animals tomorrow. 10 cases admitted. MWB	
"	28.11.17		Routine as usual. 30 animals transferred sick from BOISLEUX-AU-MONT to No 7 Veterinary Hospital FORGES-LES-EAUX. 11 cases admitted. No 23015 Pte Arthington granted leave to Eng. A.D.V.S. visited section. MWB	
"	29.11.17		Routine as usual. 2 cases admitted. MWB	
"	30.11.17		Routine as usual. 2 cases admitted. Conducting party reported back. Parade all ranks for pay.	

MW Bainbridge Capt a.V.C.
O.C. 14th Mob. Vet. Sect.

CONFIDENTIAL

WAR DIARY
OF
44ᵀᴴ M.V.S.
34ᵀᴴ DIVISION

From 1.12.17 to 31.12.17.

Army Form C. 2118

WAR DIARY
or
INTELLIGENCE SUMMARY
(Erase heading not required.)

Instructions regarding War Diaries and Intelligence Summaries are contained in F. S. Regs., Part II. and the Staff Manual respectively. Title Pages will be prepared in manuscript.

Place	Date	Hour	Summary of Events and Information	Remarks and references to Appendices
S.16.a.S.q Sheet 51.3.	1.12.17		Routine as usual. No. 118114 Pte Thom & a reported from leave. 2 cases admitted	WB.
" "	2.12.17		Routine as usual. Arrangements made with R.V.O. BOISLEUX-AU-MONT for evacuation of sick animals to morrow. 3 cases admitted	WB.
" "	3.12.17		Routine as usual. 1 w basis transferred sick from BOISLEUX-AU-MONT to Hospital FORGES-LES-EAUX. 6 cases admitted	WB.
" "	4.12.17		Routine as usual. No 22931 Pte Jauss. & No 22967 Pte Munro granted leave to England. 1 case admitted	WB.
" "	5.12.17		Routine as usual. 8 cases admitted	WB.
" "	6.12.17		Routine as usual. 1 case admitted	WB.
" "	7.12.17		Routine as usual. 7 cases admitted	WB.
" "	8.12.17		Routine as usual. 3 cases admitted	WB.

Army Form C. 2118

WAR DIARY
or
INTELLIGENCE SUMMARY
(Erase heading not required.)

Instructions regarding War Diaries and Intelligence Summaries are contained in F. S. Regs., Part II. and the Staff Manual respectively. Title Pages will be prepared in manuscript.

Place	Date	Hour	Summary of Events and Information	Remarks and references to Appendices
S.16.a.49 Sheet 51 B.	9.12.17		Routine as usual. No 29235 Pte Carol & No 23915 Pte Fuelbrook reported from No 2 Veterinary Hospital for duty. 6 cases admitted. MWB.	
" "	10.12.17		Routine as usual. Gen. Officer Commanding 34th Div. visited and inspected Section. 1 case admitted	
" "	11.12.17		Routine as usual. Arrangements made with R.J.O. BOISLEUX-AU-MONT for evacuation of sick animals to morrow. 15 cases admitted. MWB.	
" "	12.12.17		Routine as usual. 47 animals transferred sick to No 7 Veterinary Hospital from BOISLEUX-AU-MONT. 1 case admitted. MWB.	
" "	13.12.17		Routine as usual. Pte Atherington reported from leave. 5 cases admitted. MWB.	
" "	14.12.17		Routine as usual. Conducting parties reported 2 cases admitted. MWB.	
" "	15.12.17		Routine as usual. 3 cases admitted. MWB.	
" "	16.12.17		Routine as usual. Arrangements made with R.J.O. BOISLEUX-AU-MONT for evacuation of sick animals to morrow. 3 cases admitted. MWB.	

Army Form C. 2118

WAR DIARY
or
INTELLIGENCE SUMMARY
(Erase heading not required.)

Instructions regarding War Diaries and Intelligence Summaries are contained in F. S. Regs., Part II. and the Staff Manual respectively. Title Pages will be prepared in manuscript.

Place	Date	Hour	Summary of Events and Information	Remarks and references to Appendices
S 16 a 89 Sheet 51.3	17.12.17		Routine as usual. 16 animals transferred sick to No 7 Veterinary Hospital FORGES-LES-EAUX from BOISLEUX-AU-MONT. 13 cases admitted. WB	
	18.12.17		Routine as usual. No 78114 Pte Ward W. transferred to No 2 Veterinary Hospital for transfer to Agricultural District. Leaving Ples Jane & Munro reported from leave. 4 cases admitted. WB	
	19.12.17		Routine as usual. Dr Manson A.S.C. granted leave to England. 2 cases admitted. Conducting party reported. WB	
	20.12.17		Routine as usual. Arrangements made with OC No 50 BOISLEUX-AU-MONT for evacuation of sick animals tomorrow. 1 case admitted. WB	
	21.12.17		Routine as usual. 23 animals transferred sick from BOISLEUX-AU-MONT to No 7 Veterinary Hospital FORGES-LES-EAUX. 11 cases admitted. WB	
	22.12.17		Routine as usual. 2 cases admitted. WB	
	23.12.17		Routine as usual. Conducting party reported. 9 cases admitted. WB	
	24.12.17		Routine as usual. 9 cases admitted. WB	

WAR DIARY
or
INTELLIGENCE SUMMARY

Army Form C. 2118

Place	Date	Hour	Summary of Events and Information	Remarks and references to Appendices
S.16.a.8.q. Sheet 51/3	25.12.17		Christmas Day. Routine as usual. WB	
" "	26.12.17		Routine as usual. WB	
" "	27.12.17		Routine as usual. Arrangements made with P/S/G BOISLEUX-AU-MONT for evacuation of sick animals to morrow. 2 cases admitted. WB	
" "	28.12.17		Routine as usual. 30 animals transferred sick from BOISLEUX-AU-MONT to No 7 Veterinary Hospital FORCES-LES-EAUX. 2 cases admitted. WB	
" "	29.12.17		Routine as usual. 6 cases admitted. WB	
" "	30.12.17		Routine as usual. Conducting party reported 1 case admitted. WB	
" "	31.12.17		Routine as usual. Parade all ranks for pay. 10 cases admitted.	

W. Bainbridge / Capt. A.V.C.
O.C. 44 Mob: Vet: Sect.

Vol 25

CONFIDENTIAL

WAR DIARY
OF
44TH M.T.S
34H DIVISION

FROM JAN 1ST 1918 to JAN 31ST 1918

Army Form C. 2118

WAR DIARY
or
INTELLIGENCE SUMMARY

(Erase heading not required.)

Instructions regarding War Diaries and Intelligence Summaries are contained in F.S. Regs., Part II. and the Staff Manual respectively. Title Pages will be prepared in manuscript.

Place	Date	Hour	Summary of Events and Information	Remarks and references to Appendices
16 a.E.q.	1.1.18		Routine as usual. Arrangements made with R.T.O BOISLEUX-AU-MONT for the evacuation of sick animals to-morrow. 1 case admitted.	
" "	2.1.18.		Routine as usual. 14 cases transferred sick by rail from BOISLEUX-AU-MONT to No.7 Veterinary Hospital FORGES-LES-FAUX. 10 animals put through Sulphur Chamber. 6 cases admitted	
" "	3.1.18		Routine as usual. No 10241 Pte Macey granted leave to England. Arrangements made with R.T.O BOISLEUX-AU-MONT for the evacuation of sick animals to-morrow. 5 cases put through sulphur chamber, 11 cases admitted.	
" "	4.1.18		Routine as usual. 22 cases transferred sick by rail from BOISLEUX-AU-MONT to No.7 Veterinary Hospital, FORGES-LES-FAUX. No.1432905 Dr Maheson A.S.C. reported from leave, 10 cases put through Sulphur Chamber, conducting party reported back. 9 cases admitted	
" "	5.1.18		Routine as usual. 10 cases put through sulphur chamber. 1 case admitted.	
" "	6.1.18.		Routine as usual. No 28305 Pte Ward & No 28141 Pte Singleton reported for duty from No 2 Veterinary Hospital, 10 cases put through sulphur Chamber, 7 cases admitted	
" "	7.1.18		Routine as usual. No 29235 Pte Caird & No 23915 Pte Ludmoor transferred to No 2 Veterinary Hospital HAVRE for duty. 10 cases put through sulphur chamber. 1 case admitted. Conducting party reported	

Army Form C. 2118

WAR DIARY
or
INTELLIGENCE SUMMARY
(Erase heading not required.)

Instructions regarding War Diaries and Intelligence Summaries are contained in F.S. Regs., Part II. and the Staff Manual respectively. Title Pages will be prepared in manuscript.

Place	Date	Hour	Summary of Events and Information	Remarks and references to Appendices
S.16.a.8.9.	8.1.18.		Routine as usual. 10 cases put through Sulphur Chamber. Arrangements made with R.T.O. BOISLEUX-AU-MONT for the evacuation of sick animals to-morrow. 3 cases admitted. No 9038 Pte Allen reported for duty from No 2 Veterinary Hospital.	
"	9.1.18		Routine as usual. 15 cases transferred sick by rail from BOISLEUX-AU-MONT to No. 7 Veterinary Hospital FORGES-LES-EAUX. 10 cases put through Sulphur Chamber. 6 cases admitted.	
"	10.1.18		Routine as usual. 8 cases put through Sulphur Chamber, 6 cases admitted.	
"	11.1.18		Routine as usual. Conducting party reported back.	
"	12.1.18		Routine as usual. 8 cases put through Sulphur Chamber, 2 cases admitted.	
"	13.1.18		Routine as usual, 5 cases put through Sulphur Chamber. Arrangements made with R.T.O. BOISLEUX-AU-MONT for the evacuation of sick animals to-morrow. 4 cases admitted.	
"	14.1.18		Routine as usual. 20 cases transferred sick by rail from BOISLEUX-AU-MONT to No.7 Veterinary Hospital. FORGES-LES-EAUX.	
"	15.1.18		Routine as usual. Commenced building new fire & sulphur box at Sulphur Chamber, old one very unsatisfactory. All now(?) medically examined & placed in categories "A" or "B". 8 cases admitted	

WAR DIARY or INTELLIGENCE SUMMARY

Army Form C. 2118

(Erase heading not required.)

Place	Date	Hour	Summary of Events and Information	Remarks and references to Appendices
S.16.c.8.q.	16.1.18		Routine as usual. One of Sulphur box in chambers finished & found to work more satisfactorily than old one, getting a better flow of sulphur fumes with half the amount of sulphur. 3 cases admitted. No 9038 Pte ...... granted leave to England.	
" "	17.1.18		Routine as usual. Covering party reported back. 4 animals put through Sulphur Chamber. Arrangements made with R.T.O. BOISLEUX-AU-MONT for evacuation of sick animals to-morrow.	
" "	18.1.18		Routine as usual. No 10247 Pte Macey reported back from leave. 13 cases transferred sick by rail from BOISLEUX AU MONT. to No 7 Veterinary Hospital FORGES-LES-EAUX.	
" "	19.1.18		Routine as usual. 10 cases put through Sulphur Chamber. 1 case admitted.	
" "	20.1.18		Routine as usual. No 9154 Sergt Downey granted leave to England. Arrangement made with R.T.O. BOISLEUX AU MONT. for evacuation of sick animals to-morrow. 16 cases admitted.	
" "	21.1.18		Routine as usual. 20 cases transferred sick by rail from BOISLEUX AU MONT. to No 7 Veterinary Hospital FORGES-LES-EAUX. 6 cases admitted.	

WAR DIARY or INTELLIGENCE SUMMARY

Army Form C. 2118

Place	Date	Hour	Summary of Events and Information	Remarks and references to Appendices
16 a.8.9.	22.1.18		Routine as usual 10 cases put through Sulphur Chamber 9 cases admitted.	
" "	23.1.18		Routine as usual. Conducting party reported 4 cases admitted	
" "	24.1.18		Routine as usual. Rifle and equipment Inspection. Gas helmet drill. Arrangements made with R.S.O. BOISLEUX-AU-MONT for evacuation to morrow.	
" "	25.1.18		Routine as usual. 23 cases transferred sent by rail from BOISLEUX au mont to No 9 Veterinary Hospital Forges les eaux	
" "	26.1.18		Routine as usual 5 cases put through sulphur Chamber	
" "	27.1.18		Routine as usual.	
" "	28.1.18		Routine as usual. Received instructions to move Section to-morrow to ERYILLERS. Handed over billets to O.C. No11 M.V.S.	

Army Form C. 2118

WAR DIARY
or
INTELLIGENCE SUMMARY

(Erase heading not required.)

Instructions regarding War Diaries and Intelligence Summaries are contained in F.S. Regs., Part II. and the Staff Manual respectively. Title Pages will be prepared in manuscript.

Place	Date	Hour	Summary of Events and Information	Remarks and references to Appendices
S.16 a. 8.9.	29.1.18		Reveille 6 AM. Parade 9.45 AM Marched off 9.50 AM. Arrived ERVILLERS 11.15 AM. & billeted. 2 cases received from 1/1½ M.V.S.	
ERVILLERS	30.1.18		Routine as usual 4 cases admitted	
"	31.1.18		Routine as usual 4 cases admitted	

W Dunlop Capt. A.V.C.
O.C. 4th Mtd. Vet. Sect.

CONFIDENTIAL

WAR DIARY.

OF

44TH MOBILE VETY SECTION

34TH DIVISION

From 1.2.1918 to 28.2.1918

Army Form C. 2118

WAR DIARY
or
INTELLIGENCE SUMMARY

(Erase heading not required.)

Instructions regarding War Diaries and Intelligence Summaries are contained in F. S. Regs., Part II. and the Staff Manual respectively. Title Pages will be prepared in manuscript.

Place	Date	Hour	Summary of Events and Information	Remarks and references to Appendices
ERVILLERS	1.2.18		Routine as usual. No 403E. Pte Allen R reported from leave. 2 cases admitted	
"	2.2.18		Routine as usual. 1 case admitted	
"	3.2.18		Routine as usual. No 9164 Pte Higgins J granted leave to England. 1 case admitted	
"	4.2.18		Routine as usual.	
"	5.2.18		Routine as usual. Sandbaths made. All ranks paraded for clothing inspection and Gas Helmet drill. 1 case admitted	
"	6.2.18		Routine as usual. 9 cases admitted	
"	7.2.18		Routine as usual. Arrangements made with R.S.O. ACHIET-LE-GRAND for evacuation of sick animals to-morrow. 1 case admitted	
"	8.2.18		Routine as usual. 20 cases transferred sick from ACHIET-LE-GRAND to No 7 Vet. Hosp. FORGES-LES-EAUX. Received orders to move Section to Reserve Area	
"	9.2.18		Reveille 5.30 A.M. Parade 9 A.M. Marched off 9.15 A.M. Arrived BERLES AU BOIS 3.30 P.M. & billeted	

1875 Wt. W593/826 1,000,000 4/15 J.B.C. & A. A.D.S.S./Forms/C. 2118.

WAR DIARY or INTELLIGENCE SUMMARY

Army Form C. 2118.

Place	Date	Hour	Summary of Events and Information	Remarks and references to Appendices
BERLES-AU BOIS	10.2.18		Reveille 5.30 AM. Parade 9.15 AM. Marched off 9.20 AM. Arrived LE-CAUROY at 3.45 PM. Y billeted	
LE-CAUROY	11.2.18		Routine as usual. Horse left behind by 2/1 N.M. M.V.S. Sq. Dis collected from French inhabitant.	
"	12.2.18		Routine as usual. 1 case admitted	
"	13.2.18		Routine as usual. Horse left by 15th R.F.S. at GRAND RULLECOURT collected from 2 cases admitted	
"	14.2.18		Routine as usual. 1 case admitted	
"	15.2.18		Routine as usual. Parade all ranks for pay. 3 cases admitted	
"	16.2.18		Routine as usual. New Horse Ambulance fetched from FREVENT, old one returned to Base Ordnance. 2 cases admitted	
"	17.2.18		Routine as usual. Arrangements made with N10 FREVENT for evacuation of sick animals to-morrow.	
ABBEVILLE	18.2.18		Routine as usual. 5 cases transferred sick from FREVENT to No 14 Vet Hosp. Rifle drill 3 PM to 4 PM. 2 cases admitted	

Army Form C. 2118.

WAR DIARY
or
INTELLIGENCE SUMMARY
(Erase heading not required.)

Instructions regarding War Diaries and Intelligence Summaries are contained in F. S. Regs., Part II. and the Staff Manual respectively. Title Pages will be prepared in manuscript.

Place	Date	Hour	Summary of Events and Information	Remarks and references to Appendices
LE CAUROY	19.2.18		Routine as usual. No9964 Pte Haggns J reported from leave. Conducting party reported from ABBEVILLE. 7 cases admitted	
"	20.2.18		Routine as usual. Musketry Drill under Lieut. G Stewart Div Musketry Officer. 1 case admitted	
"	21.2.18		Routine as usual. Musketry Drill as yesterday. Horse left by 3/4 Royal West Surrey att. 8th Div at BOQUEMAISON collected from French Intabulant. Arrangements made with R.O. FREVANT for evacuation of sick animals to-morrow. 2 cases admitted.	
"	22.2.18		14 cases transferred sick from FREVANT to No.14 Veterinary Hospital ABBEVILLE. 6 cases admitted	
"	23.2.18		Routine as usual	
"	24.2.18		Rang dull. 8.30 A.M. to 10.30 A.M. 1 case admitted	
"	25.2.18		Rang dull 9 A.M to 11 A.M. 1 case admitted	

Army Form C. 2118

WAR DIARY
or
INTELLIGENCE SUMMARY
(Erase heading not required.)

Place	Date	Hour	Summary of Events and Information	Remarks and references to Appendices
E. CAUROY	26.2.18		Riding school + instruction on fitting saddlery for men last joined section. Arrangements made with R.T.O. FREYANT for evacuation of sick animals to morrow.	
"	27.2.18		Routine as usual. 12 cases transferred excl from FREYANT to No. 4 Vet. Hospital ABBEVILLE. 5 cases admitted.	
"	28.2.18		Routine as usual. 1 case admitted	

J. Drummond. Capt. A.S.C.
O.C. 4th Mob. Vet. Sect.

CONFIDENTIAL

War Diary
of
44th Mobile Vety Section
34th Division

From 1.5.18 To 31.3.19

Army Form C. 2118

WAR DIARY
or
INTELLIGENCE SUMMARY

(Erase heading not required.)

Date of arrival in France
10 – 1 – 1916.

Instructions regarding War Diaries and Intelligence Summaries are contained in F.S. Regs., Part II. and the Staff Manual respectively. Title Pages will be prepared in manuscript.

Place	Date	Hour	Summary of Events and Information	Remarks and references to Appendices
LE CAUROY	1.3.18.		Routine as usual. Collected all sick animals remaining in Division and transferred them (9 cases) to No.14 Veterinary Hospital ABBEVILLE. Received orders to move section to forward area tomorrow.	J.C.R.
"	2.3.18		Reveille 5.30AM. Parade 8.30AM. marched off 9.30AM. Arrived at ST.AMAND 3.30PM billeted.	J.C.R.
ST AMAND	3.3.18		Reveille 5AM. Parade 8.30AM. Marched off 8.40AM. Arrived at BOIRY ST. RECTRUDE 2.PM. 9 cases taken over from 51st M.V.S.	J.C.R.
BOIRY ST RECTRUDE	4.3.18		Routine as usual.	J.C.R.
"	5.3.18.		Routine as usual. Arrangements made with P.J.6. BOISLEUX–A.V.M.S. for evacuation of sick animals tomorrow. 3 cases admitted	J.C.R.
"	6.3.18		Routine as usual. 11 cases transferred sick to No.7 Veterinary Hospital FORGES–ES–EAUX. 5 cases admitted	J.C.R.
"	7.3.18		Routine as usual. A.D.V.S VI Corps visited section. 1 case admitted	J.C.R.
"	8.3.18.		Routine as usual. No.991 Staff Sergt Harper. E granted leave to England. Gas Helmet drill	J.C.R.
"	9.3.18		Routine as usual. Gas Helmet drill. 3 cases admitted	J.C.R.

WAR DIARY
or
INTELLIGENCE SUMMARY

(Erase heading not required.)

Army Form C. 2118

Instructions regarding War Diaries and Intelligence Summaries are contained in F.S. Regs., Part II. and the Staff Manual respectively. Title Pages will be prepared in manuscript.

Place	Date	Hour	Summary of Events and Information	Remarks and references to Appendices
BOIRY ST. RICTRUDE	10.3.18		Routine as usual. Gas Helmet drill. 9 Horse Responder Instruction. Received "Careful Order" 10 P.M.	K.R.
"	11.3.18		Routine as usual. Gas Helmet drill. 6 cases transferred sick to No.7 Veterinary Hospital FORGES LES EAUX. 1 case admitted. No.10150 Corp. Cooper. 6920 Pte Bishop. 27580 Pte Evans. granted leave to England.	K.R.
"	12.3.18		Routine as usual. Gas Helmet drill. Float sent to 104th F.Ambulance for sick animal. Arrangements made with R.V.O. for evacuation of sick animals to No.7 rows. 2 cases admitted.	K.R.
"	13.3.18		Routine as usual. Gas Helmet drill. Evacuation of 7 sick animals to No.7 Veterinary Hospital. 3 cases admitted.	K.R.
"	14.3.18		Routine as usual. Gas Helmet drill. Arrangements made with R.V.O. for evacuation of sick animals to morrow. 4 cases admitted.	K.R.
"	15.3.18		Routine as usual. Gas Helmet drill. 7 cases transferred from BOISLEUX-AU-MONT to No.7 Veterinary Hospital. 2 cases admitted	K.R.
"	16.3.18		Routine as usual. Gas Helmet drill. 1 sounding admitted from No.1 dec. Ho.PAC. 3 cases admitted	K.R.
"	17.3.18		Routine as usual. Gas Helmet drill. 3 Mange cases transferred to 11 M.V.S. for evacuation. 2 cases admitted.	K.R.
"	18.3.18		Routine as usual. No. 27595 Pte Burncombe granted leave to England. 5 cases transferred sick from BOISLEUX-AU-MONT to No.7 Veterinary Hospital. 1 case admitted	K.R.

Army Form C. 2118

WAR DIARY
or
INTELLIGENCE SUMMARY
(Erase heading not required.)

Instructions regarding War Diaries and Intelligence Summaries are contained in F. S. Regs., Part II. and the Staff Manual respectively. Title Pages will be prepared in manuscript.

Place	Date	Hour	Summary of Events and Information	Remarks and references to Appendices
BOIRY ST RICTRUDE	19.3.18		Routine as usual. Float sent to 10th Royal Scots & to No 1 Dec 34th D.A.C. for sick animals. Rifle drill. Arrangements made with R.H.Q. Boisleux-Au-Mont for evacuation of sick animals to No No 7. 6 cases admitted	H.C.R.
"	20.3.18		Routine as usual. Gas Helmet drill. Float sent to 10th Entrenching Battalion for sick Horse. 7 cases transferred sick from Boisleux-Au-Mont to No 7 Veterinary Hospital	H.C.R.
"	21.3.18		Routine as usual. No 22964 Pte Munro sent to XI Corps Horse Dip for duty No 17974 Pte Smith. No 4029 Pte Stanger to No 26606 Pte Blood H. No 30610 Pte Blue H.J. reported from No Vet. Hospital to relieve H. Category D. men. 2 cases admitted.	H.C.R.
"	22.3.18		Routine as usual. Received orders to move at 15 minutes notice. 2 animals destroyed. 3 class A men sent to Railhead to proceed to HAVRE but were not able to entrain as there were no train service. Moved from BOIRY ST RICTRUDE at 2 PM Arrived at DOUCHY-LES-AYETTE 3.30 PM.	H.C.R.
DOUCHY LES AYETTE	23.3.18		Routine as usual. Gas Helmet inspection	H.C.R.

Army Form C. 2118

WAR DIARY
or
INTELLIGENCE SUMMARY
(Erase heading not required.)

Instructions regarding War Diaries and Intelligence Summaries are contained in F.S. Regs., Part II. and the Staff Manual respectively. Title Pages will be prepared in manuscript.

Place	Date	Hour	Summary of Events and Information	Remarks and references to Appendices
DOUCHY LES AYETTE	24.3.18		Routine as usual 2 cases admitted Moved from DOUCHY LES AYETTE at 1 P.M. arrived at BAVINCOURT. 9. P.M.	ACR
BAVINCOURT	25.3.18		Moved from BAVINCOURT. 9 AM arrived at ETREE WAMIN 3 P.M. Pte Munro reported for duty from 6th Corps Horse Dip	ACR
ETREE WAMIN	26.3.18		Moved from ETREE WAMIN 9.30 AM arrived at LA NEUVILLE 5 P.M.	ACR
LA NEUVILLE	27.3.18		Moved from LA NEUVILLE 1.30 PM arrived at YALHUON at 10 PM. 1 h/o Meale left unit French inhabitants no fit to travel	ACR
YALHUON	28.3.18		Moved from YALHUON 8.30 AM arrived LA-PUGNOY at 3.30 PM	ACR
LA-PUGNOY	29.3.18		Moved from LA PUGNOY 9 AM arrived ESTAIRES 4.30 P.M.	ACR
ESTAIRES	30.3.18		Moved from ESTAIRES 12.45 P.M. arrived LESTREM 3.30 PM & billetted Move completed & reported to DADVS 34th Division 6 cases taken over from HQ 4th MVS 7 cases admitted	ACR
LE-KIRLEM	31.3.18		Exercise for Section Horses 6. to 8 AM. No 997 Staff Sergt Harper No 6920 Pte Bishop No 10150 Corps Cooper No 27586 Pte Burles reported from leave.	ACR

A.C. Rockett
Capt
A.C. & H.F M.V.S.

CONFIDENTIAL

WAR DIARY
OF
44TH MVS
34TH DIV
FROM
1.4.18 TO 30.4.18

Army Form C. 2118

WAR DIARY
or
INTELLIGENCE SUMMARY
(Erase heading not required.)

Place	Date	Hour	Summary of Events and Information	Remarks and references to Appendices
LE NIRLEM	1.4.18		Routine as usual. No 19974 Pte Smith, No 26606 Pte Blood, No 23911 Pte Rub, No 4029 Pte Stanger, No 27602 Pte Webster, No 23015 Pte Arthington transferred to 15th Corps Veterinary Evacuation foulutz. Float sent to 122nd Bde R.A. 38th Div for sick animal. W.B.	
"	2.4.18		Routine as usual. No 4693 Pte Turnbull, No 27586 Pte Burke, No 30383 Pte Beet No 28114 Pte Singleton (class "A") men transferred to No 2 Vet Hospital. 6 cases admitted. W.B.	
"	3.4.18		Routine as usual. 20 cases evacuated by road to 15th Corps V.E.S. 13th Corps visited section. W.B.	
"	4.4.18		Routine as usual. 3 cases evacuated by road to 15th Corps V.E.S. 6 cases admitted. W.B.	
"	5.4.18		Routine as usual. 6 cases evacuated by road to 15th Corps V.E.S. 2 cases admitted. W.B.	
"	6.4.18		Routine as usual. 12 cases evacuated by road to 15th Corps V.E.S. 12 cases admitted. W.B.	
"	7.4.18		Routine as usual. 9 cases evacuated by road to 15th Corps V.E.S. 7 cases admitted. W.B.	
"	8.4.18		Routine as usual. 4 cases admitted. 7 cases transferred to 15th Corps V.E.S. W.B.	
"	9.4.18		Routine as usual. 9 cases admitted. Orders received to move Section in 20 minutes. Section moved to BLANCHE MAISON 5.30 PM arrived 7.30 PM billeted 11 Animals destroyed. W.B.	
BLANCHE MAISON	10.4.18		Routine as usual. Moved section to Petit sec Bois arriving 9.30 PM & billeted. W.B.	

Army Form C. 2118

WAR DIARY
or
INTELLIGENCE SUMMARY
(Erase heading not required.)

Instructions regarding War Diaries and Intelligence Summaries are contained in F.S. Regs., Part II. and the Staff Manual respectively. Title Pages will be prepared in manuscript.

Place	Date	Hour	Summary of Events and Information	Remarks and references to Appendices
PETIT SEC BOIS	11.4.18		8 cases transferred sick to 15th Corps V.E.S. Moved section 4 PM arrived BOIRE 6 PM & camped.	
BOIRE	12.4.18		Moved section from BOIRE 4.10 PM arrived MORBECQUE 10.15 PM & camped.	
MORBECQUE	13.4.18		Moved section from MORBECQUE 8.30 a.m. arrived GODWAERSVELDE 2.15 PM & camped.	
GODWAERSVELDE	14.4.18		Routine as usual. 6 cases admitted.	
"	15.4.18		Routine as usual.	
"	16.4.18		Routine as usual.	
"	17.4.18		Vicinity of camp shelled by enemy. Standing to ready to move off at short notice. 10 cases transferred sick to No 23 Veterinary Hospital ST OMER. Moved section to GODWAERSVELDE STEENVORDE road arriving 11 a.m. & billeted.	
"	18.4.18		Routine as usual. 2 cases admitted.	
"	19.4.18		Routine as usual. 8 cases transferred sick to No 22 V.E.S. WIPPENHOEK Pte Turnbull No 27586 Pte Burke returned to duty from HAYRE having been reclassified B.1. No 23015 Pte Arthington No 2391 Pte Kirk No 26606 Pte Blood No 27602 Pte Webber No 17994 Pte Smith No 4029 Pte Stanger reported from 15th Corps V.E.S.	

Army Form C. 2118

WAR DIARY
or
INTELLIGENCE SUMMARY

(Erase heading not required.)

Instructions regarding War Diaries and Intelligence Summaries are contained in F. S. Regs., Part II. and the Staff Manual respectively. Title Pages will be prepared in manuscript.

Place	Date	Hour	Summary of Events and Information	Remarks and references to Appendices
GODTAERSVELDE	20.4.18		Routine as usual. 19 Cases Evacuated by road to 22nd V.E.S. WIPPENHOEK. 13 Cases admitted. No 2391 Pte Ryal, No 2301 Pte Arthington transferred for duty to No 2 Vet. Hosp. HAVRE. WyB.	
"	21.4.18		Routine as usual. 5 Cases admitted. WyB.	
"	22.4.18		Moved from GODYAERSVELDE-STEENVORDE road at 6.30 am. arrived ST JANS-TER BIEZAN 11+5 AM. 6 Cases transferred sick to 22nd V.E.S WIPPENHOEK. WyB.	
ST. JANS-TER BIEZEN	23.4.18		Routine as usual. 3 cases admitted. Parade all ranks for pay No 1736 Pte Bright admitted to Hospital. WyB.	
"	24.4.18		Routine as usual. 1 case admitted. WyB.	
"	25.4.18		Routine as usual. 12 cases admitted. Order received to move out in 20 minutes. order afterwards cancelled. WyB.	
"	26.4.18		Routine as usual. 15 cases evacuated by road to 2nd Corps V.E.S PROVEN. WyB.	
"	27.4.18		Routine as usual. 4 cases admitted. WyB.	
"	28.4.18		Routine as usual. 4 cases admitted. WyB.	

WAR DIARY or INTELLIGENCE SUMMARY

Army Form C. 2118

(Erase heading not required.)

Instructions regarding War Diaries and Intelligence Summaries are contained in F.S. Regs., Part II. and the Staff Manual respectively. Title Pages will be prepared in manuscript.

Place	Date	Hour	Summary of Events and Information	Remarks and references to Appendices
ST JANS-TER BIEZEN	29.4.18		Reveille 4.30 a.y. Orders received to move section Marched off 10.15 a.y. arrived WATOU 12.30 PM 9 camped 9 cases transferred sick by road to 22nd C.C.S. PROVEN 6 cases admitted	MB
WATOU	30.4.18		Routine as usual 6 cases admitted 9 cases transferred sick to 2nd Corps S.C.S. PROVEN 2 cases admitted	

J. Sambirey / Capt a.v.c.

O.C. 44 M.V.S.

CONFIDENTIAL

WAR DIARY
OF
44TH M.V.S
37TH DIVISION.

FROM 1.5.18 TO 31.5.18

Army Form C. 2118

Formation of Sw. 1. M.V.S 1.5.15

WAR DIARY
or
INTELLIGENCE SUMMARY
(Erase heading not required.)

Instructions regarding War Diaries and Intelligence Summaries are contained in F. S. Regs., Part II. and the Staff Manual respectively. Title Pages will be prepared in manuscript.

Place	Date	Hour	Summary of Events and Information	Remarks and references to Appendices
WATOU	1.5.18		Routine as usual. 5 cases admitted. WB	
"	2.5.18		Routine as usual. 3 cases admitted. WB	
"	3.5.18		Routine as usual. 7 cases admitted. WB	
"	4.5.18		Routine as usual. 1 case admitted. WB	
"	5.5.18		Routine as usual. WB	
"	6.5.18		Routine as usual. 1 case admitted. WB	
"	7.5.18		Routine as usual. 3 cases transferred sick by road to No 22 V.E.S. No 20086 Pte Clegg E joined from No 14 Veterinary Hospital. WB	
"	8.5.18		Routine as usual. 1 case admitted. WB	
"	9.5.18		Routine as usual. 1 case admitted. WB	
"	10.5.18		Routine as usual. 2 cases admitted. WB	

Army Form C. 2118

WAR DIARY
or
INTELLIGENCE SUMMARY
(Erase heading not required.)

Instructions regarding War Diaries and Intelligence Summaries are contained in F. S. Regs., Part II. and the Staff Manual respectively. Title Pages will be prepared in manuscript.

Place	Date	Hour	Summary of Events and Information	Remarks and references to Appendices
WATOU	11.5.16		Routine as usual. Inspection of Rifles & Equipment. Gas helmet drill. 5 cases admitted. Orders received to move Section to back area.	
	12.5.16		Reveille 5.30 AM. 8 cases transferred over to No 22 C.C.S. Proven. Parade 9 AM. Marched off 9.15 AM. Arrived LES CLOCHES 4.15 PM & billeted	
LES CLOCHES	13.5.16		Reveille 5 AM. Parade 7 AM Marched off 7.15 AM arrived MELLES-LES-BLEQUIN 8.15 PM & billeted	
MELLES-LES-BLEQUIN	14.5.16		Routine as usual. Changed camp old site not suitable	
"	15.5.16		Routine as usual. 1 case admitted	
"	16.5.16		Routine as usual. 24 cases admitted	
"	17.5.16		Routine as usual. 25 cases (including 1 horse recommended for further training by O.R.) transferred over by road to No 23 Veterinary Hospital ST-OMER. Parade all ranks for pay. 5 cases admitted	
"	18.5.16		Routine as usual	

Army Form C. 2118

WAR DIARY
or
INTELLIGENCE SUMMARY

(Erase heading not required.)

Formation of Division 1 & 15 MTs 1 & 5

Place	Date	Hour	Summary of Events and Information	Remarks and references to Appendices
MELLES LES BLEQUIN	19.5.15		Routine as usual.	
"	20.5.15		Routine as usual. 4 OR Inoculated T.A.B.	
"	21.5.15		Routine as usual. 1 case admitted.	
"	22.5.15		Routine as usual. 1 N.C.O. + 30 OR. Inoculated T.A.B. 6 case transferred sick by road to No 23 Veterinary Hospital ST OMER.	
"	23.5.15		Routine as usual. 6 case admitted.	
"	24.5.15		Routine as usual. 1 N.C.O. + 4 OR Inoculated T.A.B.	
"	25.5.15		Routine as usual.	
"	26.5.15		Routine as usual. 1 N.C.O. + 4 OR Inoculated T.A.B.	
"	27.5.15		Routine as usual. 1 case admitted.	

Army Form C. 2118

WAR DIARY
or
INTELLIGENCE SUMMARY
(Erase heading not required.)

Instructions regarding War Diaries and Intelligence Summaries are contained in F.S. Regs., Part II. and the Staff Manual respectively. Title Pages will be prepared in manuscript.

Place	Date	Hour	Summary of Events and Information	Remarks and references to Appendices
MELLES LES BEQUIN	28.5.18		Routine as usual. 2 cases admitted. 1 NCO & 30 OR Inoculated TAB. No. 28305 Pte Ward H. admitted to Hospital.	
"	29.5.18		Routine as usual. 4 cases admitted.	
"	30.5.18		Routine as usual. 1 NCO & 1 Man Inoculated TAB. No. H527 Sergt Cent J.R. transferred to No 2 Veterinary Hospital for duty.	
"	31.5.18		Routine as usual. 8 cases transferred sick by road to No 23 Veterinary Hospital ST. OMER. Parade all ranks for Pay.	

J. Capt
O.C. 44 M.V.S.

CONFIDENTIAL

WAR DIARY

OF

44th M.T.S
34th Division

From 1.6.1918 to 30.6.1918

Army Form C. 2118

WAR DIARY
or
INTELLIGENCE SUMMARY

(Erase heading not required.)

Date of formation July 1915
July 1. 15
Armont in France 10.1.16

Place	Date	Hour	Summary of Events and Information	Remarks and references to Appendices
MÉLLÉS LES-BLÉQUIN	1.6.18		Routine as usual. Capt Bainbridge A.S.C. admitted to 10th Gen Hospital. 1 case admitted	
"	2.6.18		Routine as usual. Rifle and equipment inspection	
"	3.6.18		Routine as usual. No 28305 Pte Ward W discharged from hospital	
"	4.6.18		Routine as usual. No 28305 Pte Ward W admitted to 10 J Ambulance. 2 6 cases admitted	
"	5.6.18		Routine as usual. 3 cases admitted	
"	6.6.18		Routine as usual. 1 case (Mange) transferred sick by road to No 23 Veterinary Hospital ST.OMER	
"	7.6.18		Routine as usual. 1 case admitted. Rifle Inspection	
"	8.6.18		Routine as usual. 1 case admitted	
"	9.6.18		Routine as usual. No 40 29 Pte Stangar W admitted to 102 J Ambulance. D.S's inspected Section	

WAR DIARY or INTELLIGENCE SUMMARY

Army Form C. 2118

Place	Date	Hour	Summary of Events and Information	Remarks and references to Appendices
NIELLES LES-BLEQUIN	10.6.18		Routine as usual. No 118892 Corp Dexter & No 115114 Pte Bramley admitted to 102" Amb.	
"	11.6.18		Routine as usual. 3 cases transferred sick by road to No 23 Veterinary Hospital ST.OMER. 1 case admitted.	
"	12.6.18		Routine as usual. Inspection of Rifles, equipment and clothing. No 4029 Pte Stanger discharged from Hospital.	
"	13.6.18		Routine as usual. 2 cases transferred sick by road to No 23 Veterinary Hospital ST.OMER. No 28305 Pte Ward W. discharged from Hospital.	
"	14.6.18		Routine as usual. 6 OR transferred to No 2 Veterinary Hospital for duty, being surplus owing to reduction of M.T.S.	
"	15.6.18		Routine as usual. Capt W J Bambridge AVC changed in Hospital. 2 cases admitted.	
"	16.6.18		Routine as usual. 2 cases transferred sick by road to No 23 Veterinary Hospital ST.OMER. Orders received to move section to SAMER. 1 case admitted.	

Army Form C. 2118.

WAR DIARY
or
INTELLIGENCE SUMMARY.
(Erase heading not required.)

Instructions regarding War Diaries and Intelligence Summaries are contained in F. S. Regs., Part II. and the Staff Manual respectively. Title pages will be prepared in manuscript.

Place	Date	Hour	Summary of Events and Information	Remarks and references to Appendices
NELLES LES BLEQUIN	17.6.18		Reville 5 am. Parade 8.20 ry March off 8.30. am Arrived SAMER 2.35 PM & Camped	
SAMER	18.6.18		Routine as usual. No 1598 Cpl Dexter discharged from Hospital. 1 case admitted	
"	19.6.18		Routine as usual	
"	20.6.18		Routine as usual. Rifle & Equipment inspection	
"	21.6.18		Routine as usual.	
"	22.6.18		Routine as usual. Musketry cult 2 PM to 3.30 PM	
"	23.6.18		Routine as usual	
"	24.6.18		Routine as usual. Musketry cult 2 PM to 3.30 PM	
"	25.6.18		Routine as usual 26 cases admitted	
"	26.6.18		Routine as usual	

Army Form C. 2118.

WAR DIARY
or
INTELLIGENCE SUMMARY.
(Erase heading not required.)

Instructions regarding War Diaries and Intelligence Summaries are contained in F. S. Regs., Part II. and the Staff Manual respectively. Title pages will be prepared in manuscript.

Place	Date	Hour	Summary of Events and Information	Remarks and references to Appendices
SAMER	27.6.19		Routine as usual. 6 bases transferred out by rail to No 13 Veterinary hospital NEUFCHATEL. Group received to move section to Souveric Area tomorrow.	
"	28.6.19		Reveille 5 am. Parades 6.30 am. Movables H.5 3.35 am. Arrived ELNES 5.30 PM. Camped & Animals watered.	
ELNES	29.6.19		Reveille 5.30 am (later under) (Killer 5 a.6.) Parades left with Canal & Marché Lieutenant. One Recovery Section (?) left with Farrier and MARIE outside Parade 10.35 am. arrived ST MOMELIN at 20PM. Billetted. H/5 3.35 am, annued.	
ST MOMELIN	30.6.19		Reveille 5.30 am. Parades 6.30 am. Marched to WIZER. H.8.5 PM Billeted. H/5 3.35 am, annued.	

M. Armbridge
Capt
WVCS

CONFIDENTIAL

WAR DIARY
OF
44th M.T.S
34th DIVISION

FROM 1.7.1918 to 31.7.1918

Army Form C. 2118.

WAR DIARY
or
INTELLIGENCE SUMMARY.
(Erase heading not required.)

Place	Date	Hour	Summary of Events and Information	Remarks and references to Appendices
J13 a Cent Sheet 27.	17/7/18		Reveille 5.20 am. Parade 11.50 am & marched to entraining Station YPRES. Entrained 5 P.M.	
On Train	18/7/18		Orders received to detrain at CHANTILLY. Detrained 7.20 billeted 12.30 AM	
SENLIS	19/7/18		Reveille 3.30 am. Parade & awaiting orders 4.30 am 5 HP am arrived LARGNY 6.10 PM & billeted	
LARGNY	20/7/18		Exercise 4 to 7 am. Orders received to move Section to-morrow	
"	21/7/18		Reveille 4.30 am Parade 6 am. Marched off 6.6 am. arrived VILLERS 10 am and billeted	
VILLERS 22/7/18 MORT GOBERT PORT PORT Rd. 23/7/18			Under orders to move at once. Orders received Parade 2.15 PM. Marched off 2.20 PM arrived MORT GOBERT - LONGPORT Rd. 6.5 PM. Encamped in Woods. Routine as usual. 5 cases admitted	
"	24/7/18		Routine as usual. Horse sent to No. 5 10/20 Inf. Note for sick animal. 1 case admitted	
"	25/7/18		Routine as usual. 2 cases admitted	
"	26/7/18		Routine as usual. 1 case admitted	
"	27/7/18		Routine as usual. 11 cases from here sent by rail from VILLERS-COTTERET to 104 Vety many Hospital FORGES-LES-EAUX. 5 cases admitted	
"	28/7/18		Routine as usual. Orders received to move Section to-morrow	
"	29/7/18		Reveille 5 am. Parade 7 + 5 am arrived POZET 2.10 PM & camped. Camp not suitable so camp changed to CHOUY 2 cases admitted	
CHOUY	30/7/18		Routine as usual. 1 case admitted	
"	31/7/18		Routine as usual. 5 cases admitted	

J. Bainbridge Capt
O.C. 44 M.V.S.

WAR DIARY
or
INTELLIGENCE SUMMARY.
(Erase heading not required.)

Army Form C. 2118.

Formation of Our N.T. 5/19/8
N.T.S 1/8/19/6
Arrival in France 10.1.1916

Place	Date	Hour	Summary of Events and Information	Remarks and references to Appendices
WYLDER	1.7.18		Routine as usual Orders received to move Section to ROUSBRUGGE to-morrow. 1 case admitted.	
"	2/7/18		Reveille 5.30 a.m. Parade 6 to 7. Parade 12 to 5 P.M. March off 8.50 P.M. Arrived at ROUSBRUGGE 3.15 P.M. 1 case adm.	
ROUSBRUGGE	3/7/18		Reveille 5.30 a.m. Parade 6 to 8 a.m. Parade 12 to 5.55 P.M. March off 1 P.M. arrived at F13d central (Sheet 27) 3.10 P.M. 1 billeted 2 cases admitted	
F13d cent Sheet 27	4/7/18		Routine as usual 7 cases admitted	
"	5/7/18		Routine as usual 1 case transferred by road to No 2 US Proven	
"	6/7/18		Routine as usual 6 cases admitted	
"	7/7/18		Routine as usual 3 cases admitted No 11854 Pte Duff admitted to Hospital	
"	8/7/18		Routine as usual Rifle & Equipment inspection 1 case admitted	
"	9/7/18		Routine as usual 18 animals transferred sick by road to No 2 US & Proven 2 cases admitted	
"	10/7/18		Routine as usual	
"	11/7/18		Routine as usual 1 cat sent to 34 DVC for sick animal 2 cases admitted.	
"	12/7/18		Routine as usual 1 case admitted	
"	13/7/18		Routine as usual 11 cases admitted	
"	14/7/18		Routine as usual Orders received to be in readiness for move 18 cases transferred sick to No 2 US Proven 2 cases admitted. Sick.	
"	15/7/18		Routine as usual 3 cases Geneveuse sent to No 22 US Proven. Pte Duff invalided to England	
"	16/7/18		Routine as usual	

CONFIDENTIAL

WAR DIARY
OF
44ᵀᴴ M.T.S.
34ᵀᴴ DIVISION

From 1.8.1918 To 31.8.1918

29   44th Indian Vet Secn   Vol 33   34

Army Form C. 2118.

WAR DIARY
or
INTELLIGENCE SUMMARY.
(Erase heading not required.)

Place	Date	Hour	Summary of Events and Information	Remarks and references to Appendices
CHOUY	1.8.18		Routine as usual 5 cases admitted	
"	2.8.18		Routine as usual Orders received to move Section to move Headquarters staff for evacuation of sick animals to morrow. Received 4 aug 1st & 2nd field Squad to No 7 Vet Hospital FORGES from TIVERS-COTTRET Squad 3 months field off 5 aug arrived at OISY-SURBONE 11.0 PM	
RIPPY-SUR-BURCQ	4.5.18		Reveillé 5.30 am Squad & Services 9 am marched off 9.15 am arrived THURY 7.30 PM Billeted	
THURY	5.8.18		Reveillé 4.30 am Parade 6.15 am Squad half off 6.45 am Animals ORMS 11.30 AM Billeted 1 case admitted	
ORMOY	6.8.18		Parade 6.30 am and marched off to entraining station entrainment finished 9.20 (Lt ORMOT 11.45 PM)	
Oxhann	7.8.18		En route for ESQUELBECQ	
ESQUELBECQ	8.8.18		Arrived ESQUELBECQ 1.30 am detrained and marched to camp arriving 2.30 am 13 horse casualties	
"	9.8.18		Routine as usual 36 cases admitted	
"	10.8.18		50 animals transferred sick by road to 106 VES WLDER 46 cases admitted	
"	11.8.18		45 animals transferred sick by road to 105 VES WLDER 35 cases admitted	
"	12.8.18		34 animals transferred sick by road to 110 VES WLDER	
"	13.8.18		Routine as usual 10 usg cost seats & ST Nichole gaiters & clogs issued	
"	14.8.18		Routine as usual. Routine as usual, 1 animal transferred sick (Stout Case) to 110 2 VES WLDER space for rifle and clothing inspection	
"	15.8.18		Routine as usual	

WAR DIARY
INTELLIGENCE SUMMARY

Army Form C. 2118.

Place	Date	Hour	Summary of Events and Information	Remarks and references to Appendices
ESQUERDES	17.8.18		Routine as usual	
	18.8.18		Routine as usual. 1 case admitted	
	19.8.18		Routine as usual. 1 case admitted	
	20.8.18		Routine as usual. 1 case admitted	
			Routine usual. No.4693 Cpl Turnbull J. 3573 SS Bellinger granted leave to England. Case transferred sick by road to No.2 V.B.S. WIMEREUX. Orders received to move section to MOVINNE	
	21.8.18		Wells say Tongue 7.15 am marched off. 7.30 am arrived at/F13Cl Cent. Sheet 27. 10 am and billetted.	
F13Cl Cent	22.8.18		Routine as usual. 1 case admitted.	
Sheet 27	23.8.18		Routine as usual. 13 Cases transferred sick by road to No.2 V.B.S. PROVEN. 26 cases admitted. Pte Wards reported from leave.	
	24.8.18		Routine as usual. 30 cases transferred sick by road to No.2 V.B.S. PROVEN. 28 cases admitted.	
	25.8.18		Routine as usual. 29 Cases transferred sick by road to No.2 V.B.S. PROVEN. Base admitted	
	26.8.18		Routine as usual. 16 Cases transferred sick by road to No.2 V.B.S. PROVEN. Case admitted.	
	27.8.18		Routine as usual. 15 N° 9 am In:18qu reported to undergo a 10 course of instruction. Stable management. 2 cases admitted. 12 cases transferred sick to No.1 V.B.S. PROVEN.	
	28.8.18		Routine as usual. No.11892 Cpl Deakin H. McNichol reported from leave. Return to Course General Stable Routine 10 cases admitted.	
	29.8.18		Return to Course on fears & feeling of Annual Stable routine. 133 Remount arrived. 22 issued by No.2 V.B.S. to other Units. Sr Wallace returned to duty. Corp. Deakin beat to 9/62 Bde RFA relieving Sergt. arrangement made to move section to MOPEAU. 1 case admitted.	
	30.8.18		Return as usual feeling to course on fitting Saddlery.	
F26cl.S2	31.8.18		Parade/4.5 am marched off. 5 am arrived 27/f.26.2.3.2 taking over from H.1 M/S. Place what directive. In Wet field. Felling. No. Made dressful to Course. 2 Cases admitted	
27/f26cl.S2	9.1.8		Routine as usual feeling to course on fitting Saddlery & Cases admitted	

WAR DIARY
or
INTELLIGENCE SUMMARY.

(Erase heading not required.)

Army Form C. 2118.

Instructions regarding War Diaries and Intelligence Summaries are contained in F. S. Regs., Part II. and the Staff Manual respectively. Title pages will be prepared in manuscript.

Date of formation of Unit 1.5.15
" " " " " " " " " " " " " " " " of MTS 1.5.15
" " " " " " " " " " " " " " " " of MT5 1.5.15
Arrival in FRANCE 11.1.16

Place	Date	Hour	Summary of Events and Information	Remarks and references to Appendices
CHOCQUES	1/8/18		Routine as usual. 5 bases admitted	
	2/8/18		Routine as usual. Orders received to move. Section to morrow. Arrangements made for evacuation to morrow. 1 base admitted	
	3/8/18		Reveille 4 am. Parade 6 am. 1st bagge train from VIEHERS COTTERET to Not I/O Hospital FORGES. Section arrived BILLY-SYR-OURCQ 11 am. 2nd bagge	
BILLY SUR OURCQ	4/8/18		Reveille 5.30 am. Parade 9 am. Marched off 9.15 am. arrived THURY 7/10 PM. 1 killed	
THURY	5/8/18		Reveille 4.30 am. Parade 6.15 am. Marched off 6.26 am. arrived ORMOY 11.20 am. 1 base admitted	
ORMOY	6/8/18		Parade 6.20 PM. and marched to entraining station. Entrainment finished 12.0 AM. Train left ORMOY 11 H.P.	
ON TRAIN	7/8/18		En route for ESQUELBECQ	
ESQUELBECQ	8/8/18		Arrived ESQUELBECQ 1.30 am. Detrained and connected camp 2.30 am. 15 bases admitted	
	9/8/18		Routine as usual. 36 bases admitted	
	10/8/18		50 animals transferred each by road to No 8 V.E.S MYRDER 48 bases admitted	
	11/8/18		48 animals transferred each by road to No 8 V.E.S MYRDER 35 bases admitted	
	12/8/18		34 animals transferred each by road to No 8 V.E.S MYRDER 2 bases admitted	
	13/8/18		Routine as usual. 1 base admitted. No 11 Sqdn Lt/Col Doolin & Lt. Nicholls granted	
	14/8/18		Routine as usual. 1 base admitted	
	15/8/18		Routine as usual. Animal transference 2/Lt (Hoot Case) to T.O. 8 V.E.S MYRDER Rifle Equipment inspection	
	16/8/18		Routine as usual	

WAR DIARY / INTELLIGENCE SUMMARY

Army Form C. 2118.

Place	Date	Hour	Summary of Events and Information	Remarks and references to Appendices
ESQUENBECQ	17/8/18		Routine as usual 1 case admitted	
	18/8/18		Routine as usual 1 case admitted	
	19/8/18		Routine as usual 1 case admitted	
	20/8/18		Routine as usual 3 cases transferred out by road to No 57 C.C.S. EYLDER Batty 3 Corp Himself No 3537 L/Cpl Railway granted leave England	
	21/8/18		Reveille 5 am, Parade 7.15 am Marched off, 30 am arrived F.13 cent Sheet 27. 11.30 am 9 killed	
F.13d cent	22/8/18		Routine as usual 1 case admitted	
	23/8/18		Routine as usual 328 cases admitted 19 Cases transferred out to No 2 V.B.S PROPER No 2 & 305 Pte Ward reported from leave	
	24/8/18		Routine as usual 30 Cases transferred out to No 2 V.B.S. PROPER 2.8 Cases admitted	
	25/8/18		Routine as usual 39 Cases transferred out to No 2 V.B.S PROPER 35 cases admitted	
	26/8/18		Routine as usual 16 cases transferred out to No 2 V.B.S PROPER, 15 cases admitted	
	27/8/18		Routine as usual 10. N.C.O reported from Inf Brigade but 10 days course of instruction 2 cases admitted 2 cases transferred out to No 2 V.B.S PROPER	
	28/8/18		Routine as usual Corp Docli & 157 Nicholls Porter from leave returned to Styles Routine 1/- Lenne grain ration 16 cases admitted	
	29/8/18		Returned to Corps on Leave learning governing instruction & general state routine 133 Remount arrived and 25 issued, 16 Limbs by 12 A.S.D., 4 cap seats sent to 01/52 Battery R.F.A to act as AVC Sergt arrange for remounts to move to morrow at 6 am Goals a 157 Nicholls Porter from leave transferred to No 2 V.B.S PROPER 11 cases admitted	
	30/8/18		Parade 7.4.a.m Marched off 5am arrived R27/26 a 3.2 taking with one from H 3, 1910 L/Cce WC Mr Shelton was Field lecture to cover around frontline Routine on usual feeling to horses on fitting saddlery 4 cases admitted	
	31/8/18			

D.G.W. Mg, Capt A.V.C

CONFIDENTIAL

War Diary
of
44th M.V.S
34th Div"

From 1.9.1918 to 30.9.1918

WAR DIARY
or
INTELLIGENCE SUMMARY

Army Form C. 2118.

Formation of M.F.S. 1, 5, 10
Arrival in France 19.1.16

Place	Date	Hour	Summary of Events and Information	Remarks and references to Appendices
27/R26a32	1.9.18		Routine as usual 8 cases trans ferred over by road to No 2 V.E.S PROVEN 5 cases admitted	
"	2.9.18		Routine as usual. Orders received to move the line. New site selected at 2.34.b.07. Parade 2.30 PM arrive at new camp at 4.5 PM	
134.D.07	3.9.18		Routine as usual, 1 case admitted	
"	4.9.18		Routine as usual. No 1157 Pte E Callaghan reported for duty from YO 2 Vet Hospital. 3 cases admitted	
"	5.9.18		Routine as usual. 3 cases admitted, 8 cases trans ferred over by road to No 2 V.E.S. PROVEN	
"	6.9.18		Routine as usual. Floor sent north. 1 case to No 2 V.E.S PROVEN 1 case admitted	
"	7.9.18		Routine as usual. 10 YbO having finished a course in store & lable Management returned to their respective tlank for duty. 6 cases admitted	
"	8.9.18		Routine as usual 6 cases transferred to No 2 V.E.S PROVEN. Rifle Inspection	
"	9.9.18		Routine as usual. 3 cases admitted. 6 cases transference sick by road to No 2 V.E.S PROVEN	

Army Form C. 2118.

WAR DIARY
or
INTELLIGENCE SUMMARY.
(Erase heading not required.)

Instructions regarding War Diaries and Intelligence Summaries are contained in F. S. Regs., Part II, and the Staff Manual respectively. Title pages will be prepared in manuscript.

Place	Date	Hour	Summary of Events and Information	Remarks and references to Appendices
L34.b.07	10.9.18.		Routine as usual 19 V.S. visited Section 3 cases admitted	
"	11.9.18		Routine as usual 7 cases transferred sick by road to No 2 V.E.S PROVEN 3 cases admitted	
"	12.9.18.		Routine as usual A.D.V.S. & IX Corps visited section 6 cases admitted Rifle & Equipment inspection	
"	13.9.18.		Routine as usual 9 cases transferred sick by road to No 2 V.E.S. PROVEN.	
"	14.9.18.		Routine as usual.	
"	15.9.18.		Routine as usual 3 cases admitted	
"	16.9.18.		Routine as usual, 3 cases admitted, 13 cases transferred sick by road to No 10. V.E.S. GODEWAERSVELDE Orders received to move to morrow to L' Bombrigge, granted leave.	
"	17.9.18.		Reveille 5 am Parade 7 am Marched off growing new camp 9.15 am 9 billeted	
R14.a.96. Sheet 27	18.9.18		Routine as usual A.D.V.S. visited section 3 cases admitted	
"	19.9.18.		Routine as usual 3 N.C.O.'s & 30 O.R. reported from Inf. Base to undergo 10 days course of Horse & Stable management. 6 cases transferred sick to No 10 V.E.S. 3 cases admitted	

Army Form C. 2118.

WAR DIARY
or
INTELLIGENCE SUMMARY.
(Erase heading not required.)

Instructions regarding War Diaries and Intelligence Summaries are contained in F. S. Regs., Part II. and the Staff Manual respectively. Title pages will be prepared in manuscript.

Place	Date	Hour	Summary of Events and Information	Remarks and references to Appendices
R.H.d.q.6. Sheet 27.	20.9.15		Routine as usual. 5 cases admitted	
"	21.9.15		Routine as usual 8 cases admitted. 5 cases transferred sick by road to No 10.V.E.S.	
"	22.9.15		Routine as usual 8 cases admitted 9 cases transferred sick by road to No 10 V.E.S.	
"	23.9.15		Routine as usual 2 cases admitted, Rifle & Equipment Inspection	
"	24.9.15		Routine as usual No 11702165 Sgt Taylor J granted leave to Eng & 1 case admitted	
"	25.9.15		Routine as usual 7 cases admitted, 5 cases transferred sick by road to No 10 V.E.S.	
"	26.9.15		Routine as usual 2 SS 10th Corps Judged section 11 cases admitted. 5 cases transferred sick by road to No 10 V.E.S. Rifle inspection.	
"	27.9.15		Routine as usual 5 cases admitted	
"	28.9.15		Routine as usual No 22931 Pte Lane W sent to 14Dly Amb for Dental Treatment 4 cases admitted. 5 cases transferred sick to No 10 V.E.S.	
"	29.9.15		Routine as usual 4 cases transferred sick by road to No 10 V.E.S. 1 case admitted	
"	30.9.15		Routine as usual 6 N6 Damen from Inf. was returned to duty to their respective Units. Course of Stable Management funded 2 cases transferred sick	

WAR DIARY
INTELLIGENCE SUMMARY

Army Form C. 2118.

4th M.V.S.
October 1918

Vol. 3. No. 6

Place	Date	Hour	Summary of Events and Information	Remarks and references to Appendices
R.4.d.9.6. (Sheet 27)	1st		Routine as usual.	
"	2nd		Routine as usual. 1 Case Tranfusive Sent to No 10 V.E.S. 1 N.C.O. & 2 men established at Collecting Post at H.36.J.25. Sheet 28.	
"	3rd		Routine as usual. 6 Cases admitted. 1 Destroyed	
"	4th		Routine as usual. A.D.V.S. visited Section	
"	5th		Routine as usual. 5 Cases transferred sick to No 10 V.E.S. 19 Cases admitted	
"	6th		Routine as usual. 19 Cases transferred sick to No 10 V.E.S. 3 Cases admitted	
"	7th		Routine as usual. 4 Cases admitted	
"	8th		Routine as usual. 13 Cases admitted. Float sent to Collecting Post for sick animals. 7 Cases transferred to No 10 V.E.S.	
"	9th		Routine as usual. 9 Cases admitted. Float sent to Collecting Post for sick animals. 10 Cases transferred sick to the 10 V.E.S.	

WAR DIARY or INTELLIGENCE SUMMARY

Army Form C. 2118.

October 1918 — (Sheet 2)

Place	Date	Hour	Summary of Events and Information	Remarks and references to Appendices
R.4.d.9.6. (Sheet 27)	10th		Parade 8.30 — marched off to 26/H.36.2.0.9 & pitched Camp. 13 Cases admitted	
H.36.d.0.9. (Sheet 28)	11th		Cleaning up Camp. 11 Cases Transferred sick to No 7 V.E.S. Collecting Post recalled Section being in advance of it.	
"	12th		Routine as Usual. 10 Cases Transferred to No 7. V.E.S. 7 Cases admitted	
"	13th		Routine as Usual. 7 Cases Transferred to No 7. 22.E.S. 10 Cases admitted Float sent to ZANVOORDE to collect them.	
"	14th		Routine as Usual. 10 Cases Transferred to No 7. V.E.S. 1 Case admitted	
"	15th		Routine as Usual. 10 Cases Transferred to No 7. V.E.S. 12 Cases admitted D.D.V.S. 2 Army & A.D.V.S 10 Corps Visited Section.	
"	16th		Routine as Usual. 7 Men from 9th Transport Unit reported for 10 days Course in Horse Management. 4 Cases admitted. 4 Cases Transferred to No 10 99.E.S. D.A.D.V.S. office to day moved to this Section.	
"	17th		Marched off. 9. A.M. Arrived at R.2.A.9. a thousand Oft. — R. left at own site as guide for Remounts.	
K.31.B.2.8. (Sheet 28)	18th		Moved off 9. A.M. Arrived K.31. b. 2.2. & bivouacked. 4 Cases admitted Remounts moved at Refilling Point.	

Army Form C. 2118.

WAR DIARY
or
INTELLIGENCE SUMMARY.

(Erase heading not required.)

October 1916 (Sheet 3)

Place	Date	Hour	Summary of Events and Information	Remarks and references to Appendices
K.3, H.2.2. (Sheet 28)	19th	—	Routine as usual. 4 Cases admitted, 1 mule destroyed	
"	20th	8 A.M.	Moved off 8 A.M. Arrived Q.5.c.1.1. & Brimeaux. 6 Cases Evacuated to No 10 V.E.S.	
Q.5.c.1.1 (Sheet 26)	21st	—	Routine as usual. 1 Case admitted. Rifle & Kit Inspection	
"	22nd	8.30 P.M.	Parade 8.30 P.M. Marched to Lauwe & Billeted. 4 Cases admitted	
Lauwe (Sheet 29)	23rd	—	Routine as usual. A.D.V.S. visited Section. 6 Cases admitted	
"	24th	—	Routine as usual. A.D.V.S. visited Section. 12 Cases transferred to No X V.E.S.	
"	25th	—	Routine as usual. Clipping of Section Horses Commenced. 2 Cases admitted. 1 Case Kicked to No X V.E.S.	
"	26th	—	Routine as usual. 3 Cases evacuated. Stable management finished. 103 B Bde men returned to Units. Come. O. Stables held up on account of Division moving	
"	27th	—	Routine as usual. Parade for inspection of Gas Helmets, Kits & etc. 2 Cases admitted	
"	28th	9.30 A.M.	Moved off 9.30 A.M. from Lauwe to H.3.c.1.0. & Billeted. Remainder of Inf Bde Transport men returned to their Units. 2 Cases admitted. 7 Cases transferred to No X V.E.S.	

Army Form C. 2118.

WAR DIARY
or
INTELLIGENCE SUMMARY.

(Erase heading not required.)

October 1918
(Sheet 4)

Place	Date	Hour	Summary of Events and Information	Remarks and references to Appendices
H.S. e.1.0. (Sheet 29)	29th		Routine as usual. Parade for Inspection of Rifles & Equipment	
"	30		Routine as usual. 17 Sick Cases admitted. 1 Mule Died. Capt W.J. Bainbridge admitted to 102 Field Ambulance suffering from Influenza.	
"	31		Routine as usual. Flock sent to Collect have left at Farm (R/F). 9.2.a.3.3 17 Cases transferred to No. 2, 29 E.S. 11 Cases admitted. D.A.D.V.S. returned from leave & took over charge of M.V.S.	

M. Weatherup
D.A.D.V.S.
34th Divn.

CONFIDENTIAL

WAR DIARY
OF
44th MTS
34th DIV
FROM
1.11.1918 TO 30.11.1918

WAR DIARY or INTELLIGENCE SUMMARY

Army Form C. 2118.

FORMATION. OF M.V.S. 1-8-'15
ARRIVAL IN FRANCE 10·1-'16

Place	Date	Hour	Summary of Events and Information	Remarks and references to Appendices
HARLEBEKE	Nov 1st 1918		Routine as usual. Horse sent to Vibrator Control. 9 Animals & 1 Hide Transferred to No 2 P.E.S. 1 Case admitted	ACR
"	2nd "		Routine as usual. D.V.S. 2nd Army & ADVS 2nd Corps visited Section. 1 Case Floated from Seerlich & 1 Case Floated from AFA 2 Corps to Section. 7 Cases Transferred to No 2 P.E.S. 20 Cases admitted	ACR
"	3rd "		Parade 9 AM. Moved off from Msp. Ref. H 5.a.10 arrived at MOORSEELE & Billeted	ACR
MOORSEELE	4th "		Routine as usual. Clenny. M. Campo & Repinny. Stables. Pte. O. Callaghan A.V.C. Pte Griffin 1/5 No S.H. absent from Camp. 9-30 P.M. 7 Cases admitted	ACR
"	5th "		Routine as usual. Pte O. Callaghan & Pte Griffin reported for duty at 7-30 A.M. Pte Griffin returned to his Unit by order of D.A.D.V.S. Pte Edwards A.V.C. returned from leave to England. Reported sick & was admitted to 102 mt Field Amb. same day. 4 Cases admitted	ACR
"	6th "		Routine as usual. 1 Case returned to duty. 10 Cases Transferred to No 9 P.E.S. 6 Cases admitted to station	ACR

Army Form C. 2118.

WAR DIARY
or
INTELLIGENCE SUMMARY.
(Erase heading not required.)

Place	Date	Hour	Summary of Events and Information	Remarks and references to Appendices
MOORSEELE	Nov 7 1918		Routine as usual. Refreshing Gothics etc. A.C.R.	
"	8 "		Routine as usual. Laundry collected from Bn. A.C.R. 8 Cases transferred to No 7 V.E.S. 2 Cases admitted	
"	9 "		Routine as usual. 1 Case admitted A.C.R.	
"	10 "		Routine as usual. Attached men returned to their Units on Completion of Course of instruction in Stable Management etc. 7 Cases admitted. Pte O. Callaghan A.V.C. broke bounds while undergoing 7 days. C.13. Striking horse & rider with him A.C.R.	
"	11 "		Routine as usual. O/C Capt W.J. Bainbridge Stka Command. B Section from DAD.V.S. 19th Pte J. Franks reports for duty from 102 Field Amb. Pte Munro granted 14 days team to England. 2 Cases Redward to duty. & 1 Case admitted A.C.R.	
"	Nov 12 "		Routine as usual. Pte O. Callaghan sentenced to 28 days F.P. No 2 for breaking bounds & Remount Cases admitted to Section & Evacuated to No 2 V.E.S. 7 Cases transferred to No 7 V.E.S. 2 Cases admitted A.C.R.	
"	13 "		Routine as usual. Pte O. Callaghan sent to 1/1 Christian to complete 28 days F.P. No 2. S/Sgt Morton & Pte Jeaves returned to duty. 2 Cases reported for duty 3 Cases admitted A.C.R.	

Army Form C. 2118.

WAR DIARY
or
INTELLIGENCE SUMMARY.
(Erase heading not required.)

Place	Date	Hour	Summary of Events and Information	Remarks and references to Appendices
MOORSEELE	March 14 1918		Routine as usual. 1 Groundling admitted & transferred to No 2 D.E.S. for Pulmonary reasons. 27 Cases transferred to No 2 D.E.S. 1 admitted. JCR	22 Cases
"	" 15 "		Parade 8. A.M. moved off to WATRIPOINT arrived 7 P.M. & Billeted. JCR	
WATRIPOINT	" 16 "		Routine as usual. Clearing Stables & c. Sr. Mason A.S.C. returned from leave to England. JCR	
"	" 17 "		Routine as usual. Sr. Mason reported sick. admitted to Hospital. JCR	
"	" 18 "		Parade 7. A.M. Moved off/to LESSENES. arrived 2 P.M. & Billeted. JCR. Clearing Stables etc. Capt W.B. Bainbridge	
LESSENES	" 19 "		Routine as usual. O/C admitted to Convalescent Hospital. JCR	
"	" 20 "		Routine as usual. 1 Case floated from WODECQ & admitted. JCR	
"	" 21 "		Routine as usual. 1 Case floated from FLOBECQ 4 Cases admitted JCR	
"	" 22 "		Routine as usual. 5 Cases evacuated to No 2 D.E.S. 1 Case admitted. JCR	

Army Form C. 2118.

WAR DIARY
or
INTELLIGENCE SUMMARY.
(Erase heading not required.)

Instructions regarding War Diaries and Intelligence Summaries are contained in F. S. Regs., Part II. and the Staff Manual respectively. Title pages will be prepared in manuscript.

Place	Date	Hour	Summary of Events and Information	Remarks and references to Appendices
LESSINES	May 23rd 1918		Routine as usual. ACR	
"	24th "	"	Routine as usual. ACR	
"	25th "	"	Routine as usual. No. 2470 Pte Budgen AVC reported for duty from No 2 Hospital Home. Dr Bridges returned to 229 Coy ASC. Relief Dr Wallace ASC. 2 Cases admitted ACR	
"	26th "	"	Routine as usual. 1 Case floated from OIGNIES. 1 Case collected from 29th DIVISION. 3 Cases evacuated to No 2 B.V.S. ACR	
"	27th "	"	Routine as usual. Pte Munro AVC returned from leave to England. 2 Cases admitted ACR	
"	28th "	"	Routine as usual. 2 Cases admitted ACR	
"	29th "	"	Routine as usual. 1 Case admitted ACR	
"	30th "	"	Routine as usual. 1 Case floated from BASILLY. 2 Cases admitted ACR	

Army Form C. 2118.

WAR DIARY
or
INTELLIGENCE SUMMARY.
(Erase heading not required.)

Place	Date	Hour	Summary of Events and Information	Remarks and references to Appendices
LESSINES	1.12.18		Routine as usual. 1 Case returned to duty. 1 Case admitted.	
"	2.12.18		Routine as usual.	
"	3.12.18		Routine as usual. 1 Case Collected belonging to 7th Canadian Field Dressing Station admitted.	
"	4.12.18		Routine as usual. 1 Case admitted. No. 17974 Pte Smith A.L. granted leave to England. 5 Cases Evacuated to No 10 D.E.S.	
"	5.12.18		Routine as usual. 1 Case admitted.	
"	6.12.18		Routine as usual. 3 Cases Evacuated to No 10 D.E.S. 2 Cases admitted.	
"	7.12.18		Routine as usual. 1 Case admitted.	
"	8.12.18		Routine as usual. 1 Case admitted.	
"	9.12.18		Routine as usual. 1 Case admitted. 2 Cases Evacuated or 3 Hikes to No 10 D.E.S.	
"	10.12.18		Routine as usual. 3 Cases Evacuated to No 10 D.E.S. 2 Cases admitted. No. 1157 Pte O.Callaghan reported to Sister on Completion of 28 days of P.H.o.2. with 1/7 Cheshires	

Army Form C. 2118.

WAR DIARY
or
INTELLIGENCE SUMMARY.
(Erase heading not required.)

Instructions regarding War Diaries and Intelligence Summaries are contained in F. S. Regs., Part II. and the Staff Manual respectively. Title pages will be prepared in manuscript.

Place	Date	Hour	Summary of Events and Information	Remarks and references to Appendices
LESSINES	11-12-18		Routine as usual. 9/157 Pte O'Callaghan, E., transferred to No 2 Dist Hosp HAVRE according to instructions contained in Officer i/c R.A.P.C. records (Paris) - No T12/740/19 dated 15-11-18. MB	
"	12-12-18		Parade 8 A.M. & march off from LESSINES. arrived at SOIGNIES 2 P.M. & Billeted. MB	
SOIGNIES	13-12-18		Routine as usual. MB	
"	14-12-18		Routine as usual. MB	
"	15-12-18		Routine as usual. MB	
"	16-12-18		Parade 8-45 A.M. moved off from SOIGNIES arrived at COURCELLES. 4.30 P.M & Billeted. MB	
COURCELLES	17-12-18		Routine as usual. No 30010 Pte Clin, H. rendered to 7 Hyg - C.C. H? absence off line of march. MB	
"	18-12-18		Parade 9.30 A.M. moved off from COURCELLES, arrived at CHATELET 3 P.M & Billeted MB	
CHATELET	19-12-18		Parade 7 A.M. moved off from CHATELET arrived at SART - ST. LAURENT 10-30 A.M. & Billeted. MB	

Army Form C. 2118.

WAR DIARY
or
INTELLIGENCE SUMMARY.
(Erase heading not required.)

Instructions regarding War Diaries and Intelligence Summaries are contained in F. S. Regs., Part II. and the Staff Manual respectively. Title pages will be prepared in manuscript.

Place	Date	Hour	Summary of Events and Information	Remarks and references to Appendices
SART ST. LAURANT	20-12-18		Routine as usual.	
"	21-12-18		Routine as usual.	
"	22-12-18		Routine as usual.	
"	23-12-18		No 30310 Pte Clar H. admitted to Hospital	
"	24-12-18		Parade 9.AM. moved H from SART. ST. LAURANT. arrived at FLOREFFE & Billited.	
FLOREFFE	25-12-18		Routine as usual.	
"	26-12-18		Routine as usual. 1 Mule collected from CHATLET & admitted. No 24710 Pte Budgen J. admitted to Hospital. No 17914 Pte Smith A returned from leave to England.	
"	27-12-18		Routine as usual. Horse collected from Billet. No 25. SUARLEE. 1 Case R.T.D. 8 Cases admitted. No 10247 Pte Macey E granted leave to U.K. 1 Case collected from ST. MARTIN. 11 Cases admitted	
"	28-12-18		Routine as usual. - 2 Cases admitted.	
"	29-12-18		Routine as usual. - 2 Cases admitted.	
"	30-12-18		Routine as usual. 19 Cases Evacuated to No 4 V.E.S. 1 Case R.T.D. No 9038 Pte Allen R. granted leave to England. 17 Cases admitted including 10 Cases from 4 Canadian M.V.S. 11 ͭ ͪ Canadian Division	
"	31-12-18		Routine as usual - 2 Cases admitted	

CONFIDENTIAL

WAR DIARY

OF

44th MVS

Army Form C. 2118.

WAR DIARY
or
INTELLIGENCE SUMMARY.
(Erase heading not required.)

Instructions regarding War Diaries and Intelligence Summaries are contained in F. S. Regs., Part II. and the Staff Manual respectively. Title pages will be prepared in manuscript.

Place	Date	Hour	Summary of Events and Information	Remarks and references to Appendices
FLOREFFE	1-1-19		Routine as usual - 2 Cases admitted	
"	2-1-19		Routine as usual - 1 Case admitted	
"	3-1-19		21 Cases Evacuated including 10 Animals - M.V.S. 4th Canadian Division - To No 10 B.E.S. 1 Case admitted to 4th Canadian	
"	4-1-19		Routine as usual. 2 Cases admitted	
"	5-1-19		Routine as usual.	
"	6-1-19		Routine as usual. 10 Cases admitted	
"	7-1-19		Routine as usual. 3 Cases admitted	
"	8-1-19		Routine as usual. 6 Cases admitted	
"	9-1-19		Evacuation of 26 Sick Animals to No 10 B.E.S. 2 Case admitted	
"	10-1-19		Routine as usual. Conducting party reported back from CINEY. 3 Travelling admitted	
"	11-1-19		Routine as usual - 5 Cases admitted	
"	12-1-19		Routine as usual. 2 Cases admitted	
"	13-1-19		Routine as usual.	
"	14-1-19		Routine as usual. 1 Case floated from St. GERARD to Section & other Cases admitted No 3637 S/Smith BELLINGER W. admitted sick to 104 Field Ambl.	

WAR DIARY
or
INTELLIGENCE SUMMARY.
(Erase heading not required.)

Army Form C. 2118.

Place	Date	Hour	Summary of Events and Information	Remarks and references to Appendices
FLOREFFE	15-1-19		Routine as usual. 14 Cases Evacuated to Adv. Vety. Hosp. CHARLEROI. 11 Animals Class D - & 7 Class D - admitted. 4 Mules sent to A.V. Hosp.	
"	16-1-19		Routine as usual. 3 Sick Cases admitted.	
"	17-1-19		11 Animals Class D - & 3 Sick Cases Transferred to No. 4 V.E.S. and 9 Animals sent to NAMUR for Brothery - & Sick Cases admitted.	
"	18-1-19		Routine as usual. 1 Case admitted.	
"	19-1-19		Routine as usual. 4 Sick Cases & 3 Class D - and - Class D - admitted.	
"	20-1-19		Routine as usual. 1 Sick Case & 1 Class D - admitted. No 997 S/Sergt HARPER.E & No 22931. Pte FAUX.W. admitted to 4 C.C.E.S.	
"	21-1-19		Routine as usual. 3 Sick Cases admitted. 1 Class D & 2 D - admitted. No 22043 Pte Earl.J. No.27272 Pte Halleron & 35429 Pte Dollintin. T. reported for duty from No 2 Vety. Hosp HAVRE	
"	22-1-19		Routine as usual. 18 Sick Cases & 6 Class D - Transferred to No 4 V.E.S. 2 Mules sent to No 4 V.E.S. & 2 Cases admitted.	

WAR DIARY
or
INTELLIGENCE SUMMARY.
(Erase heading not required.)

Army Form C. 2118.

Place	Date	Hour	Summary of Events and Information	Remarks and references to Appendices
FLOREFFE	23-1-19		Routine as usual. 4 Criminals Class D sent to NAMUR for Butchery. 4 Sick Cases admitted.	
"	24-1-19		Routine as usual. 4 Cases Transferred to No 4 99 E.S. 2 Cases admitted.	
"	25-1-19		Reveille 5-30.A.M. Moved off from FLOREFFE & entrained for Germany. 2 Sick Cases left with Inhabitants at No 4 Billet. Cpl Turnbull granted Leave to England. Sevemont - FLOREFFE.	
SIEGBURG	26-1-19		Arrived at TROISDORF. Marched to SEIGBURG. Billeted.	
"	27-1-19		Routine as usual. 1 Case admitted. No 27595 Pte Brimcombe admitted to 104 Field Ambulance.	
"	28-1-19		Routine as usual. (Moved from Billet - SEIGBURG to factory next to D.H.Q in LUSENSTRASSE.	
"	29-1-19		Routine as usual. 2 Cases admitted. No 11087 S/B Stewart. J. reported for duty from No 2 G.H. HAVRE	
"	30-1-19		Routine as usual. A.D.V.S. X Corp. inspected Section. No 4141 Sergt. HORNBY. W.H. reported for duty from Vet. Stny Hospital at CHARLEROI. 4 Cases admitted.	
"	31-1-19		Routine as usual. 3 Sick Cases, 2 Horses Class D admitted to Section.	

J.W.Bainbridge
0.1.44 M.V.S.T. car A.Q.S.C

CONFIDENTIAL

WAR

DIARY

OF 44 MVS.

MONTH

ENDIND

FEB. 28. 1919

WAR DIARY
or
INTELLIGENCE SUMMARY.
(Erase heading not required.)

Army Form C. 2118.

Place	Date	Hour	Summary of Events and Information	Remarks and references to Appendices
SIEGBURG	1-2-19		Routine as usual. – 1 Horse R.T.D. – 3 Sick cases & 4 animals Class D. admitted	WB.
"	2-2-19		Routine as usual. – 1 Horse R.T.D. – 4 Sick cases admitted.	WB.
"	3-2-19		Routine as usual. – 1 Animal Class D & 2 Sick cases admitted. 4 Animals Class D. sent to Abattoirs COLOGNE.	WB.
"	4-2-19		Routine as usual. – 4 Sick animals admitted.	WB.
"	5-2-19		Routine as usual. – 2 Sick animals admitted. – 15 Sick Animals transferred to No 10. V.E.S. No 27586 Pte BURLES F.C. to Concentration Camp COLOGNE for demobilization.	WB.
"	6-2-19		Routine as usual. – 2 Sick Animals & 1 Class D admitted. No 342.37. Pte GREAVES. W.N. & 9705. Pte GRUNDY. J. reported for duty from No 2 Vety Hospital – 2 Animals Class D sent to Abattoirs COLOGNE.	WB.
"	7-2-19		Routine as usual.	WB.
"	8-2-19		Routine as usual. – 7 Sick animals admitted – 8 Sick animals – transferred to No 10 V.E.C.	WB.
"	9-2-19		Routine as usual.	WB.
"	10-2-19		Routine as usual. – 1 Sick Animal admitted – No 9760 P.HIGGINS.J. reported to Section for duty from leave to England.	WB.
"	11-2-19		Routine as usual. – 1 Sick Animal admitted.	WB.

WAR DIARY
or
INTELLIGENCE SUMMARY.

(Erase heading not required.)

Army Form C. 2118.

Instructions regarding War Diaries and Intelligence Summaries are contained in F. S. Regs., Part II. and the Staff Manual respectively. Title pages will be prepared in manuscript.

Place	Date	Hour	Summary of Events and Information	Remarks and references to Appendices
SEIGBURG	12-2-19		Routine as usual — 2 Sick Animals admitted.	
"	13-2-19		Routine as usual — 6 Sick Animals transferred to No 10 V & E.S.	
"	14-2-19		Routine as usual — No 4693. Cpl. TURNBULL.W. reported for duty from leave to England.	
"	15-2-19		Routine as usual — 7 Sick Animals & 3 Animals Class D admitted	
"	16-2-19		Routine as usual — 1 Sick Animal admitted. No 27595 Pte BRIMICOM13E.C. reported for duty from 103rd Field Ambulance.	
"	17-2-19		Routine as usual — 1 Sick Animal admitted — 8 Sick Animals transferred to No 10. V.E.S. — 3 Animals Class D sent to Abattoir COLOGNE.	
"	18-2-19		Routine as usual — 1 Sick Animal admitted — 1 Animal Class D sent to No 10 V.E.S. for distruction by orders ADVS. X Corps.	
"	19-2-19		Routine as usual — 3 Sick Animals admitted.	
"	20-2-19		Routine as usual — 6 Sick Animals admitted.	
"	21-2-19		Routine as usual — 2 Sick Animals admitted — 11 Sick Animals transferred to No. 10. V. & E.S.	
"	22-2-19		Routine as usual — 2 Sick Animals admitted.	

Army Form C. 2118.

WAR DIARY
or
INTELLIGENCE SUMMARY.
(Erase heading not required.)

Instructions regarding War Diaries and Intelligence Summaries are contained in F. S. Regs., Part II. and the Staff Manual respectively. Title pages will be prepared in manuscript.

Place	Date	Summary of Events and Information	Remarks and references to Appendices
SEIGBURG	23.2.-19	Routine as usual — 1 Sick Animal admitted — No 8788 Pte MARSDEN. N. No 6113 Pte ROBSON. N. & No 13267 Pte RICHARDSON. JN. reported for duty from No 2 Vety Hospital — HAVRE.	
"	24.2.-19	Routine as usual — 1 Sick Animal admitted — Dr WALLACE.E. J. granted leave to England — fourteen days. Via CALAIS	
"	25.2.-19	Routine as usual — Dr McCULLUN. W. reported for duty from 229 C.A.S.C. Temp. 17 Animals Class Z & 1 Class D — admitted — 3 Sick Animals admitted	
"	26.2.-19	Routine as usual — 17 Animals Class Z & 1 Class D — sent to slaughter COLOGNE. — 4 Sick Animals admitted.	
"	27.2.-19	Routine as usual — 11 Sick Animals Transferred to No 10. V.E.S. No 27595 Pte BRIMICOMBE.G. granted 14 days leave to England. VIA. CALAIS	
"	28.2.-19	Routine as usual — 1 Sick Animal admitted.	

W Bowling
T. Capt. R.Q.V.C.
O.C. 4 M.V.S.

CONFIDENTIAL

WAR DIARY.

Unit. 44. M.V.S.

Month Ending
March 31st, 1919

WAR DIARY
or
INTELLIGENCE SUMMARY.
(Erase heading not required.)

Army Form C. 2118.

OFFICER-IN-CHARGE RECORDS
16 APR 1919
ROYAL ARMY VETY. CORPS.

Instructions regarding War Diaries and Intelligence Summaries are contained in F. S. Regs., Part II. and the Staff Manual respectively. Title pages will be prepared in manuscript.

Place	Date	Hour	Summary of Events and Information	Remarks and references to Appendices
SIEGBURG	1-3-19		Routine as usual. — No 8785 Pte. MARSDEN, admitted to No 104 Field Ambulance and 3. O.R. returned to No 2 Rest Hospital. HAVRE. — 31 Animals Class Z admitted.	/B
"	2-3-19		Routine as usual. — 1 Sick Animal admitted. 32 Animals Class Z/2 sent to WIMSON COLOGNE. 10	/B
"	3-3-19		Routine as usual. — 1 Case admitted.	/B
"	4-3-19		Routine as usual. — 1 Sick Animal + 6 Class. Z. admitted.	/B
"	5-3-19		Routine as usual. — 3 Sick Animals + 14 Class Z admitted.	/B
"	6-3-19		Routine as usual. — 20 Animals Class Z sent to Stratford COLOGNE.	/B
"	7-3-19		Routine as usual. — 1 Sick Animal + 8 Animals Class Z admitted.	/B
"	8-3-19		Routine as usual. — No 8785 Pte MARSDEN reported for duty from 104 Field Ambulance. — 9 Sick Animals transferred to No 10. V.E.S. — 3 Sick animals and 4 Animals Class Z admitted.	/B
"	9-3-19		Routine as usual. — No T/6871 A/S. STEWART.J. and 13267 Pte RICHARDSON.J. sent to 2nd Army Concentration Camp COLOGNE for demobilization. — 1 Sick and 14 Class Z animals admitted.	/A
"	10-3-19		Routine as usual. — 1 Sick Animal admitted. — 20 Animals Class Z sent to COLOGNE for destination.	/A
"	11-3-19		Routine as usual. — 1 Sick Animal Transferred to No 10 V.E.S. 2 Sick animals admitted. No. 26435. Pte. BREATT.W. + 31733 Pte CONLAN.J. reported for duty from No. 5 Rest Hospital. ABBEVILLE.	/B

Army Form C. 2118.

WAR DIARY
or
INTELLIGENCE SUMMARY.
(Erase heading not required.)

Instructions regarding War Diaries and Intelligence Summaries are contained in F. S. Regs., Part II. and the Staff Manual respectively. Title pages will be prepared in manuscript.

Place	Date	Hour	Summary of Events and Information	Remarks and references to Appendices
SEIGBURG	12-3-19		Routine as usual — 4 Sick Animals admitted.	A
"	13-3-19		Routine as usual — 2 Sick and 4 Class D/Z animals admitted.	A
"	14-3-19		Routine as usual — 10 Animals Class D/Z sent to Abattoir Cologne for Slaughter. 6 Sick Animals admitted. No 21284 Sergt. TOWLE. J. reported for duty from 41. M.V.S.	A
"	15-3-19		Routine as usual — 3 Sick Animals admitted.	A
"	16-3-19		Routine as usual — 3 Sick animals admitted. No 27593 Pte Bannister. S. reported for duty from 104 Field Ambulance. No 16920 Pte BISHOP. F. granted 14 days leave to England — No 71141 Sergt. HORNBY. W. returned for duty to No 2 Base Hospital HAVRE.	B
"	17-3-19		Routine as usual — 19 Sick animals transferred to No 10 V.E.S. — 12 Animals Class D/Z admitted. No 206654 S/S WHITLOCK. W. & No 20760 Pte MAYES. A. reported for duty from No 10 Base Hospital NEUFCHATEL.	B
"	18-3-19		Routine as usual — 1 Sick Animal transferred to No 10.V.E.S. — 4 Sick Animals admitted. 13 Animals Class D/Z sent to Abattoir COLOGNE.	B
"	19-3-19		Routine as usual. No 10150 Cpl COOPER. W. granted 14 days leave to England. No 17974 Pte SMITH. A.B. admitted to 104 Field Ambulance. 2 Sick animals admitted.	A
"	20-3-19		Routine as usual — 3 Sick Cases & 10 Animals Class D/Z admitted.	A
"	21-3-19		Routine as usual — 3 Sick Cases & 14 Animals Class D/Z admitted. Capt. W.J. BAMBRIDGE granted 14 days leave to England.	A

Army Form C. 2118.

WAR DIARY
OR
INTELLIGENCE SUMMARY.
(Erase heading not required.)

Place	Date	Hour	Summary of Events and Information	Remarks and references to Appendices
SEIGBURG	22-3-19		Routine as usual — 24 Animals Class D/Z sent to Abattoir COLOGNE for destruction. 4 Sick Animals admitted.	/s
"	23-3-19		Routine as usual — 2 Sick Cases admitted.	/s
"	24-3-19		Routine as usual — 3 Sick Cases admitted. No 9708 Pte GRUNDY. J. to 2nd Army Concentration Camp. COLOGNE. for demobilization.	/s
"	25-3-19		Routine as usual — 8 Sick Animals Transferred to No. 10 V.E.S. 2 Sick Cases and 6 Animals Class D/Z admitted.	/s
"	26-3-19		Routine as usual — 1 Sick Animal admitted - 12 Animals Class D/Z to Abattoir COLOGNE for destruction.	/s
"	27-3-19		Routine as usual — 4 Sick Animals admitted.	/s
"	28-3-19		Routine as usual — 2 Sick admitted & 6 Sick Animals Transferred to 10 V.E.S.	/s
"	29-3-19		Routine as usual — 2 Sick Animals admitted.	/s
"	30-3-19		Routine as usual — 1 Sick Animal admitted.	/s
"	31-3-19		Routine as usual — 1 Sick Animal admitted	/s

W.F.Smith.
Major
A.D.V.S. 44 M.V.S.

Army Form C. 2118.

WAR DIARY
or
INTELLIGENCE SUMMARY.
(Erase heading not required.)

Instructions regarding War Diaries and Intelligence Summaries are contained in F. S. Regs., Part II. and the Staff Manual respectively. Title pages will be prepared in manuscript.

OFFICER-IN-CHARGE RECORDS
19 MAY 1919
ROYAL ARMY V. CORPS.

Place	Date	Hour	Summary of Events and Information	Remarks and references to Appendices
SIEGBERG	1-4-19		Routine as usual — No 17974 Pte Smith. A.L. reported for duty from 103rd Field Ambulance. No 9704 W/Cpl Higgins. J. admitted to 103rd Field Ambulance — 2 Sick Animals admitted to Section. WB	
"	2-4-19		Routine as usual — 16 Animals Class D/I admitted to Section. WB	
"	3-4-19		Routine as usual — Capt J.B. Russell. R.A.V.C. assumed temporary Command of Section in absence of Capt W.J. Bainbridge — 1 Sick Animal admitted — 20 Animals Class D/I Transferred to Abattoir COLOGNE for Slaughter. WB	
"	4-4-19		Routine as usual — 2 Sick Animals admitted. WB	
"	5-4-19		Routine as usual — No 6920 Pte Bishop. F. reported for duty from leave to England. 4 Sick Animals admitted — 6 Animals Transferred to No X V.E.S. WB	
"	6-4-19		Routine as usual — No 6113 Pte ROBSON.N. & No 6785 Pte MARSDEN.N. despatched to Concentration Camp COLOGNE for demobilization — 2 Sick Animals admitted. WB	
"	7-4-19		Routine as usual — No 10150 Cpl. Cooper.H. reported for duty from leave to England. 1 Sick Animal admitted — 6 Animals Transferred to No X V.E.S. WB	
"	8-4-19		Routine as usual — 3 Sick Animals admitted. WB	
"	9-4-19		Routine as usual — Capt W.J. Bainbridge returned from leave to England. WB	
"	10-4-19		Routine as usual — No 29305 Pte WARD.H. granted 14 days leave to England — 7 Sick Animals Transferred to No X V.E.S. WB	

D. D. & L., London E.C
(1934) W1 W5300/P713 750,000 3/18 E 688 Forms/C2118/6.

WAR DIARY
or
INTELLIGENCE SUMMARY.
(Erase heading not required.)

Army Form C. 2118.

Instructions regarding War Diaries and Intelligence Summaries are contained in F. S. Regs., Part II. and the Staff Manual respectively. Title pages will be prepared in manuscript.

Place	Date	Hour	Summary of Events and Information	Remarks and references to Appendices
SIZBURG	11-4-19		Routine as usual — The following O.Rs. Numbers 16779 Pte ROWE. A. 18080 Pte TURNER. J. 19305 Pte SKADE. E. 23606 Pte WILKINSON G. 26292 Pte ENEVER. H.G. and Pte R7017 SOLOMON G.D. reported for duty from 2/1 West Lancs M.V.S. — No 9764 A/Cpl HIGGINS. reported for duty from 103rd Field Ambulance. NUB	
"	12-4-19		Routine as usual — 2 Sick Animals admitted to Section. NUB	
"	13-4-19		Routine as usual — No 26435 Pte BREATT. W. admitted to 103 Field Ambulance. 1 Sick Animal admitted to Section. NUB	
"	14-4-19		Routine as usual — 3 Sick Animals admitted to Section. NUB	
"	15-4-19		Routine as usual — 4 Sick Animals admitted to Section — 6 Animals transferred to No X. V.E.S. NUB	
"	16-4-19		Routine as usual — 2 Sick Animals admitted to Section. NUB	
"	17-4-19		Routine as usual — 3 Sick Animals admitted to Section — 5 Animals transferred Sick to No X. V.E.S. NUB	
"	18-4-19		Routine as usual — 1 Sick Animal admitted to Section. NUB	
"	19-4-19		Routine as usual. NUB	
"	20-4-19		Routine as usual — No 4693 Cpl TURNBULL. W. No 9764 A/Cpl HIGGINS. J. and No 6920 Pte BISHOP. F. despatched to 2nd Army Concentration Camp COLOGNE. for demobilization. NUB	

Army Form C. 2118.

WAR DIARY
or
INTELLIGENCE SUMMARY.

(Erase heading not required.)

Instructions regarding War Diaries and Intelligence Summaries are contained in F. S. Regs., Part II. and the Staff Manual respectively. Title pages will be prepared in manuscript.

Place	Date	Hour	Summary of Events and Information	Remarks and references to Appendices
SIEGBURG	21-4-19		Routine as usual — No 26435 Pte BREATT. W. reported for duty from No 102 Field Ambulance — 3 Sick Animals admitted to Section.	
"	22-4-19		Routine as usual — 1 Sick Animal admitted to Section.	
"	23-4-19		Routine as usual — 1 Sick Animal admitted to "	
"	24-4-19		Routine as usual — 2 Sick Animals admitted to " — 6 Animals Transferred to No X V.E.S.	
"	25-4-19		Routine as usual — No 20760 Pte MAYES. A. granted 14 days leave to England from 29-4-19 to 12-5-19.	
"	26-4-19		Routine as usual — 1 Sick Animal admitted — No 17974 Pte SMITH.A.6. despatched to 2nd Army Concentration Camp. COLOGNE for demobilization.	
"	27-4-19		Routine as usual —	
"	28-4-19		Routine as usual — No 26-305 Pte WARD.W. reported for duty from leave to England	
"	29-4-19		Routine as usual — 5 Mules sent to Army Slaughtering. COLOGNE.	
"	30-4-19		Routine as usual — 4 Sick Animals admitted to Section. 6 Sick Animals Transferred to No X V.E.S.	

O.C 44 M.V.S.

CONFIDENTIAL

WAR DIARY

OF 44th M.V.S. EASTᴺ DIVISION.

FOR MONTH ENDING APRIL 30 1919

Army Form C. 2118.

WAR DIARY
or
INTELLIGENCE SUMMARY.

(Erase heading not required.)

Instructions regarding War Diaries and Intelligence Summaries are contained in F. S. Regs., Part II. and the Staff Manual respectively. Title pages will be prepared in manuscript.

ROYAL ARMY VETY. CORPS.
9 MAY 1919

Place	Date	Hour	Summary of Events and Information	Remarks and references to Appendices
SIEGBURG	1-4-19		Routine as usual — No 17974 Pte Smith, A.L. reported for duty from 103rd Field Ambulance. No 9764 A/Cpl Higgins, J. admitted to 103rd Field Ambulance — 2 Sick Animals admitted to Section.	WJB
"	2-4-19		Routine as usual — 16 Animals Class D/Z admitted to Section.	WJB
"	3-4-19		Routine as usual — Capt J.B. Russell, R.A.V.C. resumes Kemping Command of Section in place of Capt W.J. Bainbridge — 1 Sick Animal admitted — 20 Animals Class D/Z transferred to Abattoir COLOGNE for Slaughter.	WJB
"	4-4-19		Routine as usual — 2 Sick Animals admitted.	WJB
"	5-4-19		Routine as usual — No 6920 Pte Bishop, F. reported for duty from leave to England. 4 Sick Animals admitted — 6 Animals Transferred to No X V.E.S.	WJB
"	6-4-19		Routine as usual — No 6113 Pte ROBSON. N. & No 6788 Pte MARSDEN. N. despatched to Concentration Camp. COLOGNE for demobilization — 2 Sick Animals admitted.	WJB
"	7-4-19		Routine as usual — No 10150 Cpl Cooper. H. reported for duty from leave to England. 1 Sick Animal admitted — 6 Animals Transferred to No X V.E.S.	WJB
"	8-4-19		Routine as usual — 3 Sick Animals admitted.	WJB
"	9-4-19		Routine as usual — Capt W.J. Bainbridge returned from leave to England. 3 Sick Animals admitted.	WJB
"	10-4-19		Routine as usual — No 28305 Pte WARD. W.H. granted 14 days leave to England — 7 Sick Animals Transferred to No X. V.E.S.	WJB

Army Form C. 2118.

WAR DIARY
or
INTELLIGENCE SUMMARY.
(Erase heading not required.)

Instructions regarding War Diaries and Intelligence Summaries are contained in F. S. Regs., Part II. and the Staff Manual respectively. Title pages will be prepared in manuscript.

Place	Date	Hour	Summary of Events and Information	Remarks and references to Appendices
SIEGBURG	11-4-19		Routine as usual — The following O.R. Numbers 16779 Pte ROWE A. 18080 Pte TURNER R.J. 19308 Pte WILKINSON G. 23606 Pte SKADE. E — 26292 Pte ENEVER H.G. and 27017 Pte SOLOMON G.D. reported for duty from 2/1 West Lanc. M.V.S. — No 9764 A/cpl HIGGINS. reports for duty from 103rd Field Ambulance.	
"	12-4-19		Routine as usual — 2 Sick Animals admitted to Section.	
"	13-4-19		Routine as usual — No 26435 Pte BREATT. W. admitted to 103 Field Ambulance. 1 Sick Animal admitted to Section.	
"	14-4-19		Routine as usual — 3 Sick Animals admitted to Section.	
"	15-4-19		Routine as usual — 4 Sick Animals admitted to Section — 6 Animals transferred to No X. V.E.S.	
"	16-4-19		Routine as usual — 2 Sick Animals admitted to Section.	
"	17-4-19		Routine as usual — 3 Sick Animals admitted to Section — 5 Animals transferred Sick to No X. V.E.S.	
"	18-4-19		Routine as usual — 1 Sick Animal admitted to Section.	
"	19-4-19		Routine as usual.	
"	20-4-19		Routine as usual — No 4693 Cpl TURNBULL. W. No 9764 A/Cpl HIGGINS. J. and No 6920 Pte BISHOP. F. despatched to 2nd Army Concentration Camp BOLOGNE. for demobilization.	

Army Form C. 2118.

WAR DIARY
or
INTELLIGENCE SUMMARY.
(Erase heading not required.)

Instructions regarding War Diaries and Intelligence Summaries are contained in F. S. Regs., Part II. and the Staff Manual respectively. Title pages will be prepared in manuscript.

Place	Date	Hour	Summary of Events and Information	Remarks and references to Appendices
SIEGBURG	21-4-19		Routine as usual — No 26435 Pte TREAT T.W. reported for duty from 102 Field Ambulance — 3 Sick Animals admitted to Section.	MB
"	22-4-19		Routine as usual — 1 Sick Animal admitted to Section.	MB
"	23-4-19		Routine as usual — 1 Sick Animal admitted to "	MB
"	24-4-19		Routine as usual — 2 Sick Animals admitted to " 6 Animals Trans— fered to No X V.E.S.	MB
"	25-4-19		Routine as usual — No 20760 Pte MAYES. A. granted 14 days leave to England from 29-4-19 to 12-5-19.	MB
"	26-4-19		Routine as usual — 1 Sick Animal admitted — No 17974 Pte SMITH.A.L. despatched to 2 Army Concentration Camp. COLOGNE for demobilization.	MB
"	27-4-19		Routine as usual.	MB
"	28-4-19		Routine as usual — No 26305 Pte WARD.H. reported for duty from leave to England	MB
"	29-4-19		Routine as usual — 5 Hides sent to Army Slaughtery. COLOGNE.	MB
"	30-4-19		Routine as usual — 4 Sick Animals admitted to Section. 6 Sick Animals Transferred to No X V.E.S.	MB

MJ Cowlinds ? Capt
O.C. 44 M.V.S.

CONFIDENTIAL

WAR DIARY

of

44ᵗʰ MVS

MONTH ENDING

MAY 1919

Army Form C. 2118.

WAR DIARY
or
INTELLIGENCE SUMMARY.
(Erase heading not required.)

Instructions regarding War Diaries and Intelligence Summaries are contained in F. S. Regs., Part II and the Staff Manual respectively. Title pages will be prepared in manuscript.

Officer in Charge Records
No. 2 JUL 1919
Royal Army Veterinary Corps

Place	Date	Hour	Summary of Events and Information	Remarks and references to Appendices
SIEGBURG	1-5-19		Routine as usual – 14 Sick Animals admitted.	
"	2-5-19		Routine as usual – 3 Sick Animals admitted – 16 Animals transferred to No X V.E.S.	
"	3-5-19		Routine as usual – 14 Sick Animals admitted.	
"	4-5-19		Routine as usual – .	
"	5-5-19		Routine as usual – 16 Sick Animals admitted – 27 Sick Animals transferred to No X V.E.S.	
"	6-5-19		Routine as usual – W.O. O 2165 Sgt Taylor S.G. granted leave to U.K. from 7-5-19 to 21-5-19. 5 Sick Animals transferred to No X V.E.S.	
"	7-5-19		Routine as usual – 5 Sick Animals admitted.	
"	8-5-19		Routine as usual – Bcc Respirator by Sgt B Gas. School – Rifle inspection by O.C. – 50 Sick Animals admitted.	
"	9-5-19		Routine as usual – 15 Sick admitted – 60 Animals transferred to No X V.E.S.	
"	10-5-19		Routine as usual – 10 Sick animals transferred to No X V.E.S.	
"	11-5-19		Routine as usual – 1 Sick Animal admitted.	
"	12-5-19		Routine as usual – 15 Sick Animals transferred to No X V.E.S.	
"	13-5-19		Routine as usual –	
"	14-5-19		Routine as usual – 7 Sick Animals admitted.	

Army Form C. 2118.

WAR DIARY
or
INTELLIGENCE SUMMARY.
(Erase heading not required.)

Instructions regarding War Diaries and Intelligence Summaries are contained in F.S. Regs., Part II and the Staff Manual respectively. Title pages will be prepared in manuscript.

Place	Date	Summary of Events and Information	Remarks and references to Appendices
SIEGBURG	15-5-19	Routine as usual – 10 Sick Animals admitted – 1 Animal sold to Local Butcher at SIEGBURG.	
"	16-5-19	Routine as usual – 4 Sick Animals admitted – 17 Animals transferred to No I V.E.S.	
"	17-5-19	Routine as usual – 2 Sick Animal admitted – Rifle Inspection by O.C.	
"	18-5-19	Routine as usual – 1 Horse returned to duty.	
"	19-5-19	Routine as usual – 12 Sick Animals admitted.	
"	20-5-19	Routine as usual – 1 Sick Animal admitted – 17 Animals transferred to No I V.E.S.	
"	21-5-19	Routine as usual – 1 Sick Animal admitted.	
"	22-5-19	Routine as usual – 6 Sick Animals admitted. No 20760 Pte Mages reported for duty from leave to U.K.	
"	23-5-19	Routine as usual – 1 Sick Animal admitted – 6 Animals transferred to No I V.E.S. – No 16779 Pte Rowe granted 14 days leave to England from 25-5-19.	
"	24-5-19	Routine as usual – 1 Sick Animal admitted – No 66647 Pte Williams 53rd Bedfords (attached RASC) reported for duty, for relief of No T/364233 Dr McCullum No T/62165 L/Cpl Taylor reported for duty from leave to England.	

(10342) Wt W5300/P713 750,000 3/18 E 688 Forms/C2118/16.

Army Form C. 2118.

WAR DIARY
or
INTELLIGENCE SUMMARY.
(Erase heading not required.)

Place	Date	Hour	Summary of Events and Information	Remarks and references to Appendices
SIEGBURG	25-5-19		Routine as usual – 4 Sick animals admitted – No 115-14 Pte FRANK. J.A. reported for duty from Hospital.	
"	26-5-19		Routine as usual – No 101350 2/Sgt. COOPER R.M. posted to No II V.E.S. for duty – 4 Sick animals admitted.	
"	27-5-19		Routine as usual – 2 Sick Animals admitted – 7 Animals transferred to No II V.E.S. – 1 Animal sold to Lord Bustler SIEGBURG.	
"	28-5-19		Routine as usual – 1 Animal admitted.	
"	29-5-19		Routine as usual – 5 Animals admitted – 7 O.R. reported to Lectures for course of instructions in Horse management – Lectures	
"	30-5-19		Routine as usual – 5 Animals admitted – 7 Animals transferred to No II V.E.S.	
"	31-5-19		Routine as usual – 1 Horse admitted & transferred to Old Gr. Linds. RE – No 11814 Pte FRANK. J.A. despatched to Concentration Camps COLOGNE for demobilization – ADVS II Corps inspected Sections. DDVS Army of the Rhine	

J Barnes Capt
O c ↟↟ II. V.S.

CONFIDENTIAL

WAR DIARY

OF

44 M.V.S.

FOR MONTH ENDING

JUNE 30 - 1919

Army Form C. 2118

WAR DIARY
or
INTELLIGENCE SUMMARY
(Erase heading not required.)

M.V.S. EASTERN DIVISION

Place	Date	Hour	Summary of Events and Information	Remarks and references to Appendices
SIEGBURG	1-6-19		Routine as usual — 1 Animal admitted — No 26292 Pte. ENEVER, H.J. granted 14 days leave to U.K.	
"	2-6-19		Routine as usual — 10 Animals admitted — No 27019 Cpl. SOLOMON, G.D. — No 19301 Pte. WILKINSON, G. granted 14 days leave to U.K.	
"	3-6-19		Routine as usual — 4 Sick Animals admitted — No 10802 Pte LEID, J. despatched to Concentration Camp. COLOGNE for demobilization.	
"	4-6-19		Routine as usual — 1 Animal R.T.D. — 4 Animals admitted — 14 Animals Tran to I. VES.	
"	5-6-19		Routine as usual — 6 Animals admitted.	
"	6-6-19		Routine as usual — 5 Animals admitted — 9 Animals Transferred to No I. VES.	
"	7-6-19		Routine as usual — 3 Animals admitted.	
"	8-6-19		Routine as usual — 1 Animal admitted.	
"	9-6-19		Routine as usual — 9 Animals admitted — 17.O.R. reported to Section for course of instruction in Horse + Stable management Commencing 10-6-19.	
"	10-6-19		Routine as usual — 4 Animals admitted — 16 Animals transferred to I. VES. ADVS I Corps visited w inspected Section.	
"	11-6-19		Routine as usual — 2 Animals admitted.	
"	12-6-19		Routine as usual — 3 Animals admitted.	

Army Form C. 2118.

WAR DIARY
or
INTELLIGENCE SUMMARY.
(Erase heading not required.)

Instructions regarding War Diaries and Intelligence Summaries are contained in F. S. Regs., Part II. and the Staff Manual respectively. Title pages will be prepared in manuscript.

Place	Date	Hour	Summary of Events and Information	Remarks and references to Appendices
SIEGBURG	13-6-19		Routine as usual — 7 Animals admitted.	
"	14-6-19		Routine as usual — 2 Animals admitted — 14 Animals transferred to X VES. No. M.A. 146. Pte BRIMICOMBE. G. granted 3 months furlough to U.K. on re-enlistment for 3 years.	
"	15-6-19		Routine as usual — 1 Animal admitted — No 16779 Pte ROW E.A. admitted to Hospital.	
"	16-6-19		Routine as usual — 11 Animals admitted.	
"	17-6-19		Routine as usual — 4 Animals admitted — 14 Animals transferred to X VES.	
"	18-6-19		Routine as usual — 7 Animals admitted.	
"	19-6-19		Routine as usual — 6 Animals admitted — 14 Animals transferred to X VES.	
"	20-6-19		Routine as usual — 3 Animals admitted.	
"	21-6-19		Routine as usual — 1 Animal admitted.	
"	22-6-19		Routine as usual — 1 Animal admitted — No 34237 Pte GREAVES. A. Granted 14 days leave to U.K.	
"	23-6-19		Routine as usual — 5 Animals admitted — 4 Animals transferred to X VES. No 16060 Pte TURNER. J. granted 14 days leave to U.K.	

Army Form C. 2118.

WAR DIARY
or
INTELLIGENCE SUMMARY.
(Erase heading not required.)

Instructions regarding War Diaries and Intelligence Summaries are contained in F. S. Regs., Part II. and the Staff Manual respectively. Title pages will be prepared in manuscript.

Place	Date	Hour	Summary of Events and Information	Remarks and references to Appendices
SIEGBURG	24-6-19		Routine as usual – 4 Animals admitted – 9 Animals transferred to I. VES.	
"	25-6-19		Routine as usual – 1 Animal admitted – Pte 27921.Pte MICKLETHWAITE.F.W. granted 14 days leave to U.K.	
"	26-6-19		Routine as usual – 1 Animal admitted.	
"	27-6-19		Routine as usual – 4 Animals admitted – 4 Animals transferred to I VES.	
"	28-6-19		Routine as usual –	
"	29-6-19		Routine as usual – 3 Animals admitted.	
"	30-6-19		Routine as usual – 4 Animals admitted.	

CONFIDENTIAL

WAR.

DIARY.

OF. 44 M.V.S.

FOR

MONTH.

ENDING.

JULY. 1919

Army Form C. 2118.

44TH M.V.S. EASTERN DIVISION.	
No.	Date ....

WAR DIARY
or
INTELLIGENCE SUMMARY.

(Erase heading not required.)

OFFICER-IN-CHARGE RECORDS
18 OCT 1919
ROYAL ARMY VETY. CORPS.

Instructions regarding War Diaries and Intelligence Summaries are contained in F. S. Regs., Part II. and the Staff Manual respectively. Title pages will be prepared in manuscript.

Place	Date	Summary of Events and Information	Remarks and references to Appendices
SIEGBURG	1-7-19	Routine as usual – 1 Animal admitted – 11 Animals transferred to X V.E.S. No 20762 Pte Mayes reported for duty from Hospital.	
"	2-7-19	Routine as usual – 1 Animal admitted.	
"	3-7-19	Routine as usual – 2 Animals admitted.	
"	4-7-19	Routine as usual – 2 Animals admitted – 4 Animals transferred to X V.E.S.	
"	5-7-19	Routine as usual – 3 Animals admitted.	
"	6-7-19	Routine as usual – 1 Animal returned (fit for duty) to Unit.	
"	7-7-19	Routine as usual – 3 Animals admitted – 1 Animal transferred to X V.E.S. 2 Animals returned to Units fit for duty.	
"	8-7-19	Routine as usual – 1 Animal admitted. 8 Animals transferred to No X V.E.S. 1 Mule L.D. trembling admitted to Section – from 34 M.G.B. East'n Div.	
"	9-7-19	Routine as usual – 2 Animals admitted.	
"	10-7-19	Routine as usual – 2 Animals admitted.	
"	11-7-19	Routine as usual – 2 Animals admitted.	
"	12-7-19	Routine as usual – 2 Animals admitted.	
"	13-7-19	Routine as usual – 1 Animal admitted – No 20634 Pte Westwick F.W. reported from Base to U.K.	

Army Form C. 2118.

WAR DIARY
or
INTELLIGENCE SUMMARY.
(Erase heading not required.)

Instructions regarding War Diaries and Intelligence Summaries are contained in F. S. Regs., Part II. and the Staff Manual respectively. Title pages will be prepared in manuscript.

Place	Date	Hour	Summary of Events and Information	Remarks and references to Appendices
SIEGBURG	14-7-19		Routine as usual – 4 Animals admitted – 7 Animals transferred to No I V.E.S.	WB
"	15-7-19		Routine as usual – 2 Animals admitted – 4 Animals transferred to " I. V.E.S.	WB
			4 Animals returned to their Units fit for duty.	WB
"	16-7-19		Routine as usual – 2 Animals admitted – 1 Animal returned to Unit for duty.	WB
"	17-7-19		Routine as usual – 2 Animals admitted – 3 Animals transferred to No I. V.E.S.	WB
"	18-7-19		Routine as usual – 2 Animals admitted.	WB
"	19-7-19		Routine as usual –	WB
"	20-7-19		Routine as usual – No 37921 Pte Mickelthwaite H.W. despatched to Concentration Camp. COLOGNE for demobilization.	WB
"	21-7-19		Routine as usual – 2 Animals admitted.	WB
"	22-7-19		Routine as usual – 2 Animals admitted – 10 Animals transferred to No I V.E.S.	WB
"	23-7-19		Routine as usual –.	WB
"	24-7-19		Routine as usual – 3 Animals admitted – 1 Animal returned to Unit for duty	WB
"	25-7-19		Routine as usual – 1 Animal admitted.	WB

Army Form C. 2118.

WAR DIARY
or
INTELLIGENCE SUMMARY.
(Erase heading not required.)

Instructions regarding War Diaries and Intelligence Summaries are contained in F. S. Regs., Part II and the Staff Manual respectively. Title pages will be prepared in manuscript.

Place	Date	Hour	Summary of Events and Information	Remarks and references to Appendices
SIEGBURG	26-7-19		Routine as usual — Rifle & Box Respirator inspection.	
"	27-7-19		Routine as usual —	
"	28-7-19		Routine as usual — 3 Animals admitted.	
"	29-7-19		Routine as usual — 6 Animals transferred to No I V.E.S.	
"	30-7-19		Routine as usual — 1 Animal admitted — 1 Animal returned to Unit for duty	
"	31-7-19		Routine as usual — 2 Animals admitted.	

W.J. Rawlinson Capt.
O.C. 4 M.V.S.

www.ingramcontent.com/pod-product-compliance
Lightning Source LLC
Chambersburg PA
CBHW080906230426
43664CB00016B/2741